D1523404

A GERMAN BARON

IN GRANT'S ARMY

BEING THE RECORD OF THE EXTRAORDINARY ADVENTURES
OF

FREDERICK OTTO BARON VON FRITSCH

COMPILED FROM HIS WAR RECORD IN WASHINGTON AND
HIS PRIVATE PAPERS

EDITED AND COMPILED BY

JOSEPH TYLER BUTTS

1902

Contents

INTRODUCTION

Knight-Errantry has become only an historic memory, but the chivalric spirit which created it burns as fiercely to-day in the breasts of brave men as in medieval times. The shield is now a mere mineral decoration and the spear has been superseded by the modern rifle. The sword, however, has by no means become a pruning hook. It is stronger and more trusty than ever in the defense of home, country, and honor.

Our soldiers no longer wear coats of mail, but bare their breasts to the enemy in an armor of righteous purpose, an indomitable courage and a consciousness of their own right. Faith and devotion to beauty are as deep as in the days of the Crusades, and martial spirit still finds employment in the foremost nations of the earth. Knights of old did not excel our warriors of to-day in chivalry, gallantry or courage. The present methods of warfare make danger of destruction far more hazardous than before, and it is only the lion-hearted who dare face a modern foe!

This little volume is an accurate account of the part a German nobleman played in our great Civil War. True, he is only one of many heroes who fought and bled for that great cause. Yet none can read of his matchless bravery without becoming interested in him.

He became an American citizen in 1870, and, although permanently disabled from wounds received in battle, while serving as Captain in the Volunteer Army from 1862 to 1865, he has never received adequate compensation for them from the Government. He is a Republican, but has only occasionally been an active politician and has never sought favor from government officials. Until this little book shall have been read, only friends and acquaintances, who number many hundreds, know the extent of his wonderful experience.

Crushed by a bereavement, described in the conclusion of this book, Frederick Otto Baron von Fritsch, the eldest son of his Excellency, Carl Reich's Freiherr von Fritsch, Estate Seerhausen, near Riesa, Saxony, and of his wife, Caroline, eldest daughter of Secret Counsellor von Ziegesar, came to the United States in 1856.

1

He was armed with a substantial letter of credit and with several strong personal letters; and therefore he found many acquaintances, and has ever since numbered among his friends many of the best known persons in this country and in Europe, who are only too happy to vouch for the worthiness and integrity of this unusual man.

Baron von Fritsch was born September twenty-eighth, 1834, in Weimar, Germany. He was educated by tutors and the French governess of his sisters until he was eleven years of age, when he was sent to the high school at Grimma, which was celebrated for its skillful teaching of the ancient languages. Possessing an unusual knowledge of Greek, Latin, French, Italian, German and English, he entered the military academy at Dresden, at the age of thirteen. Here the discipline was exceedingly strict and he was considered wild, unruly and spoiled. Nevertheless, at the end of a four years' course, he passed an excellent examination, and when barely eighteen was commissioned by King John of Saxony a lieutenant in the Royal Cavalry.

He soon became known as the most daring rider in the regiment and won several first prizes for his excellent horsemanship. He was also a great social favorite; many of the Saxon princesses honored him as a partner in the cotillion and his trophies of the hunt and chase testify to the fact that he was also an expert marksman.

The following is a translation of his honorable discharge from the Royal Cavalry:

In His Royal Majesty of Saxony's Military Service, Bearer of this, Frederick Otto Baron von Fritsch, has served during three years and one month as a lieutenant in the First Cavalry Regiment, and has during that period fulfilled his duties faithfully and honestly. He has conducted himself at all times to the satisfaction of his superiors.

As he has urgently begged to now be honorably discharged, His Royal Majesty has kindly decided to grant the request. To certify to the discharge, His Royal Majesty has most graciously deigned to subscribe this document with his Royal hand personally, and has ordered to have the seal of the War Department added thereto.

So done and given at Dresden.

[Seal.] Signed—Johann, Rex.

Dresden, December 1st, 1856.

VON RABENHORST, Secretary of War.

Honorable Discharge of

Lieutenant Baron von Fritsch.

The romantic story of this man's life in the new country which he had determined to make his home is replete with adventures which are exciting and full of interest. They command respect for his prowess, enthusiasm for his bravery and sympathy for his pathetic sorrow. Upon arriving in New York, he presented a letter of introduction from the banking house of Messrs. Rothschild & Sons at Frankfort-on-the-Main to Mr. August Belmont, Senior, who received him very kindly. Until the following Lent, 1857, he moved in the best society of New York. In the spring he travelled about seeking information and entertainment. At Chicago he joined a hunting party of prominent young men, and together they journeyed to the far West, where they shot many buffaloes and other large game.

That winter Baron von Fritsch returned to New York, where he found a letter from his father urging him to return home, re-enter the army, marry and prepare himself as should the eldest son and future head of the family. This he declined to do and wrote his father that he had decided to remain in the States and work his way through life as others had done. To make his parent accede more readily to this step, he deeded the large estate, Seerhausen, in Saxony, to his younger brother, Charles, who had married a very wealthy and influential young woman.

In spite of great effort, he could secure no important business position in New York. He had had no mercantile training, but was every inch a soldier. Finally, he concluded to make use of his knowledge of the German, French and Italian languages, and in order to divorce himself from his social surroundings he went to Philadelphia, where in a short time he had a profitable number of pupils. In 1858 he was engaged as Professor of Modern Languages in Princeton, N. J. In 1859 he accepted a more remunerative

3

position in the same capacity at a large female seminary in Camden, S. C.

During the summer of 1860 he took a trip by schooner from Charleston to New Orleans, and as he was anxious to study the Spanish language, he went to Vera Cruz. In the City of Mexico he had the honor of meeting the family of President Benito Juarez and they soon became great friends. When the first French intervention took place and French soldiers were landed at Vera Cruz, some of the President's generals joined them, thus becoming traitors to their country. Baron von Fritsch offered his services and was made a colonel on the staff of the commanding general. They were sent out to destroy the revolutionary troops. While charging the camp of Leonardo Marquez at sunrise, September 14, 1862, the Baron's horse was killed; his men ran away, and he was captured. He was ordered to be shot, and was saved only by the intervention of a French colonel who had just arrived with his regiment to assist the revolutionists. He was then transported to Vera Cruz and commanded to leave the country at once. He took passage on the steamer *Trent** for Southampton, but while stopping for coal at Havana, he visited the town and heard of the great Civil War in the States. He resolved to return and offer his services to the government. He sold his ticket to Southampton, and after a few weeks' stay in Havana in order to recuperate from the great hardships he had endured in Mexico and also to secure proper letters of introduction from Germany to President Lincoln, he sailed for New York.

*The same ship that nearly brought England and the Union into conflict the year before. On November 8, 1861, the USS San Jacinto, commanded by Union Captain Charles Wilkes, intercepted the British mail packet RMS Trent and removed, as contraband of war, two Confederate diplomats, James Mason and John Slidell. The envoys were bound for Britain and France to press the Confederacy's case for diplomatic recognition and to lobby for possible financial and military support.—Ed. 2016

The events of the following years are graphically told by Captain F. O. Von Fritsch in the next few chapters. All the facts and data which have here been briefly recorded have been gathered from personal recollections of his family and friends.

The succeeding narrative is a portion of the diary which he has for years diligently kept. No official report or other works form the source of any information in this book. It is published not for notoriety, vainglory or vanity, but with' the sole purpose of showing to this great Nation that our glorious Union was saved by countless heroes among captains, lieutenants, sergeants, corporals and privates—the men behind the gun—who were at times commanded by generals without experience and lacking in military genius.

Joseph Tyler Butts.

CHAPTER I

It was in Washington, on October twenty-ninth, 1862, that I called upon Baron von Geroldt, the Prussian Minister to the United States. He had formerly represented his country in Mexico, and as I had just returned from there he was highly pleased to hear the latest news. His lovely daughter had many questions to ask about the society people in the Mexican capital, and I was the hero of the day at this mansion.

His Excellency knew my father well, and I found it an easy matter to interest him in myself. He declined, however, to introduce me personally to the President and said that for the moment he did not stand very well with the Administration; besides he had been obliged to ask so many favors of Mr. Lincoln that he would not, under any circumstances, use his influence to secure commissions for European officers in the Union Army.

Just then the door opened and the butler announced: "His Excellency, Lord Lyons, representing Her Most Gracious Majesty the Queen of England."

"Delighted to see you, my Lord," said the Baron. "I hope you are well and enjoyed your stay in the country."

A long but interesting conversation took place after I had been politely introduced. I reported to Lord Lyons the latest occurrences in Mexico, and he requested me to call on him soon, to tell him more about that unfortunate republic.

"I have to hurry over to the White House," he said, rising, "as Lincoln is, no doubt, anxious to see me. Good morning, gentlemen."

"My lord," broke in the Baron, "would it be asking too much of you to take the Baron over to the White House with you and gain admittance for him? He has letters to the President, but may encounter difficulty in approaching him."

"Always ready to serve you, sir. Baron, come right along with me."

After a good deal of ceremony he made me enter his carriage first, and soon we were at the White House. An usher made way for us through the immense crowd assembled there, and we were at once admitted to President Lincoln's private office at the head of the stairs, south of the main entrance.

President Abraham Lincoln was standing near a high desk by the window; he stepped towards the Ambassador, extending his hand in a most friendly way.

"How are you, Mr. Lincoln" said Lord Lyons, unceremoniously, and the President answered:

"Glad that you have returned."

They then seated themselves on a large sofa at the left and I took a position at the door, standing straight like a grenadier, with my heels together and holding my hat against my chest.

"Well, how are things?" asked Lord Lyons.

"Worse and worse," was the reply.

"McClellan did not prove so successful as you expected?"

"On the contrary; he has disappointed me very much; he is too slow, too inactive; but I'll find some good general by and by," said Mr. Lincoln.

A reference to General George Brinton McClellan.—Ed. 2016

"The Confederates hold out well," remarked Lord Lyons.

"They cannot win, even if well backed," replied the President.

One of the most fascinating and remarkable collections of Civil War letters were those between the son and grandsons of President John Quincy Adams. Charles F. Adams was Lincoln's minister to London and Charles, Jr. was an officer in the Union Army. England clearly wanted the United States weakened, as they believed they would be if secession were successful. See The Adams Letters During the Civil War.*—Ed. 2016*

Both smiled, and Mr. Lincoln, passing his hand over his face, said: "Have you met Mr. Seward?"

"Not yet. I will have a long talk with him this afternoon; I wanted to pay my respects to you first."

Then both arose and seemed at the same time to notice me.

"I met this young warrior at the Prussian Legation," said Lord Lyons. "He is fresh from Mexico. See how sunburnt he is still. He has letters for you, and I promised Baron von Geroldt to bring him along with me. I hope you can make use of him; he looks like a soldier, and soldiers you must have. Good morning, Mr. Lincoln."

"Good morning, Lyons."

The great President seated himself again on the sofa, stretched out his arms and yawned, then he said:

"What can I do for you, young man?

"My humble request to Your Excellency is to commission me as an officer in the United States Army. I was educated at the Military Academy of Dresden and I served as an officer in the cavalry, but at my request I was honorably discharged by King John. I landed in New York in December, 1850, made a living as professor of modern languages until 1800, and I have just returned from Mexico, where I had a short military experience, was captured and forced out of that country.

"I understand that there is an English and a French intervention there; have they marched to the interior?"

"Only the French, when I left, sir."

"How long is it since you returned to the States?"

"Only a few days, sir."

"Let me see the letters you have for me."

He looked them over carelessly and inquired: "Is this Bismarck's signature?"

"It is, Mr. President. He is a friend of my father and was President of the German Diet at Frankfort, when my father represented the Saxon States as Ambassador."

"What are you, a Count or a Baron?"

"A Baron, Mr. President."

"We have already a good many in the army; some do well, others do not—still it will not hurt you to have a title, but you'd better drop it, if you want to serve under our flag."

He then rose, stepped to the high desk, placed the three letters in a large envelope on which I could read the printed address: "War Department." He then wrote below:

"Deferred to Secretary Stanton.

"Abraham Lincoln."

He made a motion for me to approach and said: "I am sorry that I can't do anything personally for you, but the President does not appoint officers in the volunteer army, except sometimes a Brigadier or Major General, and I suppose that you do not want to start in as such. But I have endorsed your letters to the Secretary of War, and you had better call on him in a day or two. He may be able to place you on some General's staff."

I appreciated the humor of the War President, made a deep bow and left. Two days later I called at the War Department.

"May I see the Hon. Edwin M. Stanton?" I inquired of a mulatto [mixed-heritage] servant at the door.

"No, sir, you can't see him," he answered, in a most arrogant tone.

"When had I better call again?"

"No use calling—he is always busy."

I looked at the impudent scamp and said: "I came here by order of President Lincoln."

"I tell you, he won't see yon, nor anybody else; can't you hear? He is busy," the fellow answered again, roughly.

The blood mounted to my head, and I said: "I will inquire from someone else, you saucy scoundrel," and, thrusting him aside with such force that he fell to the floor, I entered the first room. A very polite gentleman in citizen's clothes stepped towards me and said: "What can I do for you, sir?" I handed him my card: Frederick Otto Baron von Fritsch.

9

"I had the honor to be introduced to His Excellency, President Lincoln, by Lord Lyons," I said, excitedly, "and presented some letters. The President endorsed them and ordered me to call on the Secretary of War."

"One moment, sir. I will see if Mr. Stanton is at leisure." Returning in a few minutes, he said:

"Please walk right in, Baron." Mr. Stanton was sitting at a desk tearing up papers and throwing them into a waste basket. Without looking up he asked harshly: "What is it?"

I repeated what I had said to his clerk, and added:

"I am anxious to enter the army and beg of you to favor me with a commission to serve on some General's staff."

"I have not seen the letters which you say were endorsed by the President; they are probably on file, and, besides, I do not appoint volunteer officers. Go to some Governor. Mr. Morgan, of New York, is at Willard's now; go to him." Saying this, he rose, walked into the next room and slammed the door.

In the ante-room I was again saluted by the polite clerk, and I repeated, a little dumfounded, Mr. Stanton's words, whereupon he said:

"Just so, just so; this way, please," and, with a polite bow, he gently but firmly pushed me out. In spite of his polish I felt angry enough to serve him as I had the impudent negro, who, when he saw me getting red again, stepped out of my way with alacrity. Directly after, with more or less trepidation, I called on Governor Morgan at Willard's. He was sitting in the ladies' reception room, surrounded by officers and statesmen, all with glasses in their hands and evidently having a jolly time. I stopped at the door, the Governor noticed me and said: "Step right in, sir." I bowed low, and approached him a little embarrassed, as they were gazing at me. I said:

"Governor Morgan, I believe?"

"Yes, sir."

"I regret that I have to introduce myself, but I am a stranger in Washington. My name is Baron von Fritsch." I then related my interview with the President, my call on the Secretary and their answers.

The Governor smiled and his friends laughed right out and encouraged me to come to the point. I said:

"Would you kindly commission me in one of your regiments?"

"Well, I would like to do so. You look like a soldier, and we need all we can get, but, unfortunately, it is impossible for me to comply with your request, unless some colonel has a vacancy, and applies to me for you. Find a colonel who wants you and I will be only too glad to make the appointment."

I must have looked stunned and wearied, for I evidently created some sympathy, as several of the gentlemen offered me advice. They assured me that I could easily find a colonel and suggested that I should try to join some German regiment. I thanked them, made a military bow to the Governor and marched out.

A young man in a brand new uniform with a sword and spurs on and feeling very proud and very big, walked up and down in front of the hotel office. I approached him and said:

"I beg your pardon, General, but how can I distinguish a colonel in the American army?"

"He will have an eagle on his shoulder straps," he said, shortly, and resumed his walk.

I started down Pennsylvania avenue, and, after a few blocks, I met an officer with eagles on his shoulder straps. I took off my hat politely and said:

"Beg your pardon, Colonel, but I would like to inquire most respectfully if you have a vacancy in your regiment; I am trying hard to get a commission as an officer?"

"Sorry; I am in the commissary department, stationed here; colonels with regiments are all in the field."

I thanked him and passed on. I was hungry by this time, and soon after I entered Welker's Restaurant. By Jove! Eagles and stars on the straps of all the guests! The head waiter pulled out a chair for me at a table where sat only one officer, and he, alas, had two bars on his shoulders.

"I have just ordered an appetizer; won't you join me?" he politely asked.

"With pleasure, sir. Excuse me for not calling you by your title, but I only know that colonels have eagles."

"I am a Captain, and Aid-de-Camp."

"Glad to meet you, Captain; allow me to order the luncheon."

I treated him to the best there was, and soon we became quite friendly.

Looking around, I said: "Have none of these colonels a regiment?"

He gazed from one to another and said:

"Not one; they are all quartermasters, commissaries, or staff officers."

We then talked of the war, and finally, somewhat disheartened, I left him and walked about town.

About six o'clock I entered a German hotel, on the other side of Pennsylvania Avenue, for a glass of beer, and behold! there stood at the bar a very red faced officer, wearing eagles, and drinking champagne with five or six younger officers. By divine inspiration, or out of sheer desperation, I approached and said:

"Colonel, *wie geht's?*"

He looked at me a moment, then put his glass down and grasping both my hands with his, he exclaimed:

"*Donner und kanonen!*" (*thunder and cannons*). "When did you come over? God bless you, my dear friend. Gentlemen, here is one of my old comrades from Europe, a braver fellow never lived! I am glad to meet you—come, have a glass of wine."

He filled a glass for me and, as I noticed that the bottle was nearly empty, I ordered several more, on my own account. We drank, and I felt deeply chagrined at not being able to place the Colonel. I thought that he must have served in the Saxon Infantry, and that I had forgotten him.

In a few moments I had a chance to speak to another officer about him, and I was told that he was the Colonel of the 68th Regiment, New York Volunteers, and had formerly served in the Austrian army.

"Under what name did he enlist?" I inquired.

"His own—Bourry d'Ivernois."

The conversation I had interrupted when accosting the Colonel now returned to its former subject, and they talked about General Siegel and promotions.

Franz Sigel (1824 –1902) was a German military officer, revolutionist and immigrant who was a teacher, newspaperman, and politician.—Ed. 2016

The Colonel leaned all the while heavily on me, from time to time slapping me on the back, and repeating:

"I am awfully glad that you came over."

After a time he seemed to feel uneasy, and ordered some brandy.

He swallowed a big dose, and became quite shaky. "Let us sit down," he remarked, and I assisted him to a chair, which he came very near missing. I ordered more champagne and the Colonel reiterated to the other officers, squeezing my hand, that I was the bravest fellow he had ever known, and to me he said over and over again: "Glad to have you here, old comrade."

I thanked him, and regretted that I had no commission as yet, and could not show my bravery in America.

"I'll get you a commission, old fellow; you must serve in my regiment! I would not go back to the field without you!"

"Thanks, Colonel; do you know that Governor Morgan is right here at Willard's Hotel?"

"No, is that so? I want to see him at once."

"The Governor told me that if I could find a colonel who wanted me, he would gladly sign my appointment."

"Well, let us go over; it is only a step. I'll ask him for your commission."

I helped the Colonel, who was now in a very mellow condition, to his feet, and guided him to the Avenue.

"Better brace up, Colonel," I said.

"I'm all right; come on."

He staggered across the Avenue, and in a few minutes we were at Willard's. Just then the Governor came out of the dining-room, and I addressed him: "Governor," I said, "this is Colonel Bourry of the 68th New York Volunteers, and he has kindly offered me a position in his Regiment."

"Have you a vacancy, Colonel?" he asked.

"Yes, sir; I want this gentleman to become First Lieutenant in Company F."

The Governor turned around, and calling an officer who was probably his Adjutant General, said:

"Take this young man's name, and send him a commission as First Lieutenant, Company F, 68th New York. You can go to the field," he added, addressing me, "and in a few days the commission will reach the regiment. Glad that you succeeded so quickly."

"Governor," began the Colonel; but His Excellency probably noticed his condition, and turned away to speak to a gentleman nearby. "Let's go, Colonel," I said, gently insisting, and taking hold of his arm, I led him out of the hotel.

We ate supper at the German Hotel, and then my superior said: "I'd better turn in; I must leave for the camp early, as the Provost

Marshal is after me. Will you please order my horse at six o'clock sharp? He is at the livery stable right back of here."

"And how can I go out, Colonel?"

"Just tell the stable man to let you have a good horse, and that I will send him back by the sutler. Now, be sure to wake me at six o'clock sharp; we must start in time. Waiter, just help me upstairs."

I informed some German officers of my good luck, and one, who had just been discharged, offered me his sword and a pistol, as he said, at cost price. Then he walked with me to a store, where I bought a ready-made uniform—a rather good fit—high boots, two blankets, some woolen shirts, a cap, etc., and by ten o'clock I was pretty well equipped.

I paid my bill at Willard's Hotel and checked my trunk, packed with the citizen's outfit. By advice, I also secured a large, fine canteen, and had it filled with the best rye whiskey, bought a box of good cigars, and had a big luncheon wrapped up; then I spent the balance of the night talking to officers and ex-officers, and while treating them, getting a good deal of information.

At five I went to the livery stable and ordered the Colonel's horse to be ready at half past five. The stable man, who knew Bourry well, willingly let me have a horse for myself. Out of gratitude, I paid the Colonel's bill, along with my own, settled the Colonel's account at the hotel, and then tried to wake him.

He was lying fully dressed, on the top of his bed. I shook him and washed his face with a wet towel, but he only answered with groans.

"Get him a cocktail," said someone, and after lifting him up, we persuaded him to drink. He only groaned more, but after swallowing six cocktails, he got up, mounted his horse, and we rode away.

When we crossed the Long Alexandria Bridge, he sat very much to one side, and I offered him some whiskey out of my canteen. He took a big, deep pull, and this seemed to bring back his wits, for, after gazing at me for some time, he said:

"May I have the pleasure of knowing your name, sir?"

"My name is Otto Von Fritsch, First Lieutenant Company F, 68th Regiment New York Volunteers."

"The devil you are! And since when?"

"You asked Governor Morgan to commission me last evening."

"I did?" replied the thoroughly astonished Colonel. "Why, sir, I don't know anything about this! For God's sake, don't say a word when we reach the regiment. I have promised promotions and commissions to five or six men lately."

We reached camp about noon, and I entered the Colonel's tent with him. He kept on drinking my whiskey, without saying a, word, and then lay down on his cot and began to snore.

The Adjutant told me that Colonel Bourry was one of those unfortunate men who are never quite sober, and that he suffered terribly, if deprived of whiskey.

"He will probably keep drunk now for five or six days," he said.

The Colonel occupied two tents, and was sleeping in the rear one. I fixed a bed for myself in the front one. He talked to himself at times, and then would take another long pull.

I had ingratiated myself, during the evening, with a Captain von Haake, and confided to him my appointment. He counselled me to keep it quiet and wait for the commission. As I felt much annoyed about the Colonel, who now seemed to have attacks of delirium tremens, I moved to another tent, and never left it until the fifth day, when the Adjutant approached me, holding a large envelope in his hand, and exclaiming:

"What does this mean? Otto Von Fritsch, First Lieutenant Company F, 68th New York. There is no vacancy in that company."

"Ask the Colonel," I coolly replied.

The Colonel was dead drunk, and Haake advised me to take his horse, ride to a mustering officer, four miles off, and get mustered in the United States service. "Then they can't send you away," he added.

I did so, and the next day, seeing the Colonel standing in front of his tent, I reported for duty. The other First Lieutenant of Company F came up about the same time. The Colonel began to abuse him shamefully, calling him a coward, an incompetent officer, and even stronger names. They almost came to blows, as the Lieutenant indignantly asserted that the Colonel was drunk.

Finally he said: "Mr. Yon Fritsch can have my position. I would not serve any longer under such a brute of a Colonel; I will write my resignation at once, and accept a captaincy offered to me some time ago in the 74th Pennsylvania."

He resigned, and I was First Lieutenant of Company F rightfully, but I was not a little disgusted to serve in a regiment whose Colonel was a drunkard, and where much animosity seemed to exist among the officers.

Captain von Haake had meantime taught me the American tactics, and, from his tent, I had carefully watched the guard mounting and detachments leaving for outpost duties. I had been drilled in the tent, in the manual of arms, and I surprised the Adjutant and several officers very much by giving the correct commands, when ordered without delay on picket duty. Von Haake said that I did well, and the soldiers felt that they had to deal with a competent officer, which was, under the circumstances, of much value to me.

We remained in camp two weeks longer and then received marching orders. It so happened that on the first day's march I became quite lame, my heavy boots having rubbed the skin off my left foot. General Schimmelpfennig, passing by the Regiment, noticed it, and said: "What is the matter with your foot, Lieutenant?"

"Oh, I'll have to get acquainted with this tramping, General. I am a cavalry officer by profession, and have never walked much."

"Did you serve in Germany?"

"Yes, sir, I was an officer in the Saxon Cavalry."

"I need an Aid-de-camp who can ride well. Would you serve on my staff?"

17

"With the greatest pleasure, sir!"

"Come to see me to-night, and we will try to arrange it," he said as he left me.

Alexander Schimmelfennig (1824 –1865) was a German soldier and political revolutionary before coming to the U.S. in 1854. He and Carl Schurz raised an all-German regiment.—Ed. 2016

I called on him as soon as we struck camp, and then took the order appointing me as Aid-de-camp to Colonel Bourry. He uttered some oaths, but I did not care.

I managed that night to buy a horse and saddle from Chaplain Mussehl, and rode proudly the next day on the left of the Brigade Commander.

"I have to thank you very much for this detail, General," I said, gratefully. "I feel quite like another man on horseback; besides, I did not like things very much in the regiment in which I had enlisted."

"I can understand that very well," answered the General, "and I am glad to have you with me. You joined the army a little late. In sixty-one you could easily have started as a captain, and would probably be colonel now. At that time they needed trained officers, now thousands have had a year's experience, and in this country they know more about military affairs in one year than an officer after ten years' service in the old country. If they can hold themselves in the saddle, they consider themselves the finest riders in the world, and every sergeant, after ten months' service, thinks that he should command the regiment."

"They probably think of Napoleon, who, from a Corporal, became the greatest General the world has ever known," I suggested.

"I shall need you mostly as an inspector of outposts, Baron," resumed the General, "and as you can sketch, I beg of you to furnish me a small map of the surrounding country, whenever we take a new position. Prevent straggling on marches, and enforce discipline whenever you notice that it is lacking."

CHAPTER II.

Every day I seemed to advance in the estimation of my Commander, and he was especially friendly to me. I was contented, and considered myself in good luck. I seldom recalled the dusky beauty in Mexico, and Marie was again Queen in my thoughts. When alone in my little tent, she was with me, and my soul once more communed with hers.

"Marie," I would whisper, "my sweet bride, my guardian angel, forgive me for my infatuation in Mexico. Pray for me; ask that I may remain strong and uncrippled, and if it be God's will die like a brave soldier on the battlefield, and be allowed to join thee in those happy regions, where lovers never part again." In my sleep, I often had the sweetest dreams, after such prayers; I talked with my first, and only love, and could distinctly see her.

The 68th Infantry Regiment, of the New York Volunteers, in which I held a commission as First Lieutenant of Company F, being myself mustered in the United States service on November 1, 1862, was raised, with the permission of the Governor, by Mr. Robert J. Betge, in New York City. He called it in honor of the then Secretary of War, "The Cameron Rifles."

Beginning on the 24th day of July, 1861, in less than five weeks, twelve hundred men had enlisted, and after they had been sworn in and mustered in the United States service, the regiment left for its camping ground at Hudson City, New Jersey. From there it marched by way of Hoboken to New York, where it was embarked for Amboy and sent by rail via Philadelphia and Baltimore, to Washington, D. C. Here it was marched into a camp of instruction at Mount Pleasant, and was equipped and armed with Springfield muskets. On the 4th of September, 1861, the regiment returned to Washington, and, being drawn up in front of the White House, was presented with the United States colors by the Hon. Simon Cameron. Crossing the Potomac immediately afterwards, it went into encampment at Roach Mills, and performed its first opt-post and picket duties A scouting party of two officers and forty-five enlisted men was attacked by a Confederate force, consisting of cavalry and infantry. Four privates were shot, three of them dying soon after from their wounds at the hospital at Alexandria.

From Roach Mills the Regiment was moved to Hunter's Chapel and camped near the German Division, under the pompous General Louis Blenker. About this time there came from Albany the order to designate the regiment as the 68th New York, although it was the second regiment in the field, and it remained the whole winter in small tents doing outpost duty as far as Annandale, where one night a man was shot by an enemy outpost.

On March 10, 1862, the regiment marched to Burch Station, on the Alexandria and Orange Railroad, and reached Fairfax Courthouse after some delays occasioned by heavy rains and impassable roads. There they reported to some Major General, who ordered them at once, by way of Centreville and Manassas Junction, to Warrenton Junction, and here the Major and two Captains, while reconnoitering outside of the picket line, were captured by Confederate cavalry.

The regiment then had to march way around Warrenton, Salem, Paris, Upperville and over the Shenandoah River to Winchester, camping every night without tents on the snowy ground, or on muddy side roads for thirty-six days, when General [William] Rosecrans inspected it, and found the men dressed in rags and many without shoes. He ordered it to Petersburg, where new equipments were furnished, and General Fremont placed it under his command.

In forced marches they reached Franklin, and the officers were anxious to meet the enemy, but General Banks having retreated to Harper's Ferry, the regiment being entirely out of rations, it was ordered back to Strasburg, when it was continually surrounded and shot at by guerrillas and followed by a superior force of the Confederates.

They were then hurried over Woodstock, Eden-burg, Mount Jackson and Harrisburg to Cross Keys, where the regiment formed the reserve with the two brigades of Blenker's Division. Here Colonel Betge was placed under arrest for expressing the feelings of that much abused regiment too loudly, and for other reasons unknown to the officers. At the battle of Cross Keys, where they were under hot fire, but lost only one man, the regiment was commanded by the Lieutenant Colonel. After the battle they pursued the retreating enemy to Post Republic, then after burying the dead of other regiments, they marched to Harrisburg, Mount Jackson, Strasburg, Middletown and Cedar Creek, where the regiment came under command of General Franz Siegel, who was at that time very popular with the soldiers.

Forgetting the terrible hardships of the last months, the men cried out, feeling in better spirits: "I'll fight mit Siegel," but Siegel sent them during very hot weather, by way of Luray, to Thornton's Gap, and then back again to Luray for picket duty.

Here Betge resigned, and the Lieutenant Colonel, Klufisch, led them to Culpeper and the battlefield of Slaughter Mountain, where General Banks got the worst of it again, and went off in a hurry, leaving the burying of his dead to the 68th.

After reaching the Rapidan River, on August 18th, the 68th was marched for thirteen days in line of battle, and engaged in light skirmishes from morning until night. It defended the Waterloo Bridge and captured Sulphur Springs under heavy cannon fire. Next, it had to do picket duty on the Rappahannock River, while the Union forces were marching to Warrenton. It acted as rear guard of the army to Gainesville and Manassas, and was often shelled. On August 29th it supported the batteries and stood in heavy fire, losing an officer and four men, and then held the battlefield near Groveton during the night.

For weeks they had lived on crackers and water and there was great joy when the Commissary arrived with coffee and beans. Beans for breakfast, beans for dinner, beans for supper. "Beans, beans, beans," was the joyful song.

On the 30th of August the regiment relieved the retreating Union Army at the battle of Bull Run, and with great bravery and wonderful endurance, covered the retreat, losing eleven commissioned officers and a hundred and seventeen enlisted men.

Here Lieutenant Colonel Klufisch was severely wounded. He fell pointing to the colors of the regiment. Thirty-six shots had pierced the flag, and two color bearers had been killed when the Lieutenant Colonel grasped it, and received two shots. The Union Army kept on retreating to Centreville, Fairfax, Balls' Crossroads, and nearly to Washington.

The 68th entered Washington to bury their beloved Lieutenant Colonel, but marched right out again, and encamped near Fairfax Courthouse. From here they sent a petition to the Governor of New York to commission G. von Bourry d'Ivernois as Colonel. He had behaved well until then, they had listened to his descriptions of heroic deeds in Italy, while a captain in the Austrian army, and although they had seen him take an occasional drink, his old weakness to imbibe more than he could stand had not overtaken him. As Commander, he began at once to drink deeply, and he was in his usual condition when I ran across him at the German Hotel in Washington.

As Colonel he commanded the 68th at Thoroughfare Gap, marched it to New Baltimore, and to Centreville, where the regiment was placed in the brigade of General Schimmelpfennig, and Bourry left on a fourteen days' leave of absence for New York and the Capital. Together we had joined the regiment, and as I have stated, after two weeks, I was detailed for staff duty.

I have often been told by other officers that the 68th, when marching out of Washington, was one of the finest regiments seen up to that time. The officers were gentlemen and experienced soldiers, the men fine looking, and, considering the very short period given them to drill, marched well. The discipline was good, and the spirit excellent. Marched about, often without necessity, changed from one command to another, kept as reserve, and made to bury the dead of other regiments, reduced by different details to Provost Guards, by wounds, sickness and some desertions, the regiment, in November, 1862, when I joined it, hardly mustered six hundred men. All the original officers had been killed, or had resigned, most of the present officers were promoted volunteers, or officers from other regiments; the Colonel was drinking heavily, and the esprit du corps was bad.

Great efforts were made to fill up the regiment again, but the recruiting officers bad no success. While serving on the staff, I called one day on Colonel Bourry, and asked him to ride with me to Siegel's headquarters and see if we could not induce him to fill up the regiment with drafted men. Since I belonged to it, I was anxious that it should at least become again a creditable and noble part of the brigade.

Bourry was sober when I arrived, but insisted that he could not go, as he had no uniform. He wore a citizen's coat, an old one, with brass buttons, but it looked rough; he had a good horse, but a very poor saddle over a torn blanket, his sword was rusty and showed neglect, everything testified to the fact that his pay was used for his stomach and his throat only. He finally concluded to accompany me.

My appearance that day was in great contrast to that of Colonel Bourry. I was mounted on a magnificent bay horse, which I had bought for four hundred dollars, and baptized Caesar. He was well groomed by my excellent servant, Frankel—a former Saxon cavalry soldier. With a new English saddle over a regulation yellow trimmed saddlecloth, and a cavalry officer's bridle on his head, I believe that he was the finest looking horse in the army. I wore a blue jacket, with rich shoulder straps, which I had lately purchased while on a short leave to Washington, from Miss Kate Chase, at a soldiers' fair.

Katherine Jane ("Kate") Chase Sprague (1840 –1899) was, far more than Mary Lincoln, the Washington society hostess during the American Civil War. She was the daughter of Lincoln's ambitious Secretary of the Treasury, Salmon Chase. During the war, Kate married wealthy Rhode Island Governor William Sprague, whom she would later divorce.—Ed. 2016

I wore my Mexican riding pants, ornamented with two rows of silver buttons—lion heads, held together by silver chains—a fine steel sword, which I had formerly used in the Saxon Cavalry, and a cap trimmed with gold braid. When I rode through the camp with the Colonel, the drummer boys cried out:

"What has he got?" and the regiment answered: "Buttons, he's got!" which, in the German language, means money. I smiled, and said: "Got lots of backbone, too!" and they all laughed good naturedly.

We rode on, at a lively pace, for some three miles, when my saddle girths became a little loose, and I dismounted to adjust them, the Colonel trotting on ahead. All at once I heard: "Halt; who goes there?"

"Colonel Bourry of the 68th."

"Have you a pass?"

"No, sir; I do not need one."

"Can't pass!"

I spurred my horse, and galloped toward the picket, while the Colonel was told that the orders were that no one could reach Siegel's headquarters without a pass. The Colonel was swearing away pretty lively.

The sentinel, seeing me coming, with my outfit glittering in the bright sun, cried:

"Turn out the guard!" and the officer commanded:

"Present arms!" I saluted, and said:

"Come along, Colonel," and we rode briskly away. On the return trip, the officer told me that they had taken me for some cavalry General, and this explained the occurrence.

We soon after entered General Siegel's headquarters, located in a good sized farm house. Again I was politely saluted, and the Colonel was questioned as to how it happened that he came without being sent for, and without a pass. He got mad, and left it to me to ask the General if nothing could be done to fill up his ranks again.

"Nothing, I regret to say," answered Franz Siegel. "I am fighting all the time to get the regiments in my command filled up, but can't find a single recruit; some of the other generals seem to have the inside track in getting the drafted men, or substitutes."

24

As my promotion depended on the increase of soldiers in the regiment, I made another strong plea, but without success. Feeling very much discouraged, we mounted our horses again, after the Colonel had secured a large canteen of whiskey, and I a small sack full of canned goods, sardines and other delicacies, unknown in our brigade camp.

The Colonel took one pull after another, and his conversation soon became incoherent and most exasperating; so, when I noticed a side road, which I knew led to my camp, I said:

"Ta, ta, old comrade," and went off at full speed.

On the 10th of December we received orders to march to Dumphries and Stafford Courthouse, and then we proceeded to Falmouth, under the roar of cannons fired at Fredericksburg.

Again the Union Army suffered a terrible defeat, owing for the most part to the impassable roads, and to an attack on an impregnable position, where some regiments were cut entirely to pieces. We were not wanted, as there was nothing left for us to support, and after standing ready for action for two days and two nights, in a merciless rain and extremely cold weather, without the slightest shelter, we were ordered back again to Stafford Courthouse. After changing camp several times, we were at last allowed to pitch our tents and settle in our winter quarters, between Stafford Courthouse and Brook Station.

It was my duty to lay out the picket line and post the outposts, and I did this for the whole division. General Schimmelpfennig inspected my work, and I am proud to say, observed that no man could have done it better.

"I will let you have a run to Washington now," he said, "to get some things for our comfort."

I did not need this permission twice, and, after my short leave was approved, started at once. I shall never forget the first night in a comfortable bed again, at Willard's Hotel. How sweetly I slept and dreamed after a refreshing bath and a delicious, light supper, and how good it felt to undress and get between white sheets once more. It was Heaven!

Of course I needed money, and my capital in bank was reduced another thousand dollars in greenbacks after a week, but I was well equipped. Hiring a sutler wagon, I reached camp with folding beds, stoves, blankets, nails, chairs, cooking utensils, beer, wines and plenty of eatables

First, I fixed up the General's tent, while he was absent, then my own, and for each officer in the staff I brought an appropriate present. There was great joy, and much unexpected comfort, and my nickname for some days after was: "The Count of Monte Cristo."

Besides daily escorting the new squads to picket duty and inspecting the line once during the day and once at night, I had but little to do, and so had a chance to study the character of my General.

General Alexander von Schimmelpfennig was, in spite of his long name, a man of small stature, and slender build. His health was not good, and he suffered from dyspepsia, as a consequence of the eighteen months of hard life in the field. He was highly educated, and, after having left the Prussian service as a captain, he became by profession an engineer and splendid draughtsman. He was not sociable, and liked to be left alone, except before retiring at night. In the day time, when not feeling well, he was generally cross, and his orders were given in a sharp and very commanding voice. He was a strict disciplinarian and an excellent officer, but somewhat soured, and with no inclination to meet superior officers. He dressed in very old uniforms, and thought nothing of appearances; however, he liked to see me well dressed, and often said:

"The Baron dresses as if on parade, buttoned to the neck. It is a pleasant sight to me to see him jump fences on that fine horse of his, and he is certainly the best rider I ever saw." When I went to report, I never rode through the entrance leading to headquarters, but, to please him, always made my horse jump the surrounding' four-foot high fence. As soon as I had his orders, I dashed away at lightning speed.

At night he often came to my tent, or I entered his, and we sipped the fine tea I had brought from Washington, pouring a little arrack in it, which brightened us up and loosened our tongues. The General, to use a vulgar phrase, was not a kicker, like many other officers he always spoke kindly of superiors, and of military matters generally, sometimes regretting that things were not better, but always hoping for a good turn.

"The great misfortune and worst feature in this army is that the Generals lack experience," he said once. "They provide remarkably well, and at times most extravagantly, for the troops; they plan good campaigns; but when firing commences, or the enemy does not act as they had calculated, they lose their heads and are unable to control, assist or manoeuvre their corps. We always lack support in case of need, and reserves are never placed in the right positions. I have seen no generalship shown on the battlefield as yet. The selection of staff officers is very bad with most Generals. They detail relations, sons of old friends, or men recommended by Congressmen, and most of these latter are not scientific soldiers, have no maps, no knowledge of the country, no eyes to see where help is needed, and brigades, or regiments are left in the lurch after the attacks. But things will get better and better, and may God inspire our great President soon to pick out a commander who possesses some of Napoleon's or Moltke's genius. There is much jealousy among the Generals, and each one is anxious for personal glory and not over-anxious to assist his fellow commanders, particularly if the latter be German-Americans. So, my dear Aid, in any battle we may fight together, let us look out for ourselves, and never expect outside help. Do not even trust other German Generals. They have caught the spirit, and wish success for themselves only. Very selfish, but almost excusable in the general circumstances. I have given up all hopes of further promotion, but intend to do my duty at all times, and if possible gain some reputation for my brigade, small as it is."

On January 31, 1863, Major General Franz Siegel commanded the Eleventh Corps, Major General Carl Schurz its Third Division, and

Brigadier General Schimmelpfennig the First Brigade of that division. This brigade consisted of five regiments:

Carl Christian Schurz (1829 –1906) was a German revolutionary, American statesman and reformer, U.S. Minister to Spain, U.S. Senator, and Secretary of the Interior.—Ed. 2016

The 68th New York.............German

The 82d Illinois...............German

The 61st Ohio........................Irish

The 74th Pennsylvania....Pennsylvania German

The 157th New York............American

These regiments did alternate picket duty during the winter months, were drilled frequently, and two or three times we had a brigade drill. The regiments were all small, except the 157th, but the discipline was excellent, and in our comfortable camps, the men felt contented and were well provided for.

General Joseph Hooker had been entrusted with the command of the Army of the Potomac, to which the Eleventh Corps belonged.

One day, in the early part of April, I was inspecting as usual the picket line, when I noticed a picket running forward to the outpost. I galloped there and the Lieutenant in command reported to me that a small troop of mounted men had shown itself in front. I took my glass and saw some twelve or fifteen officers with a flag floating in the wind. I rode towards them, revolver in hand, and challenged:

"Who goes there?"

"General O. O. Howard and staff, with orders from the President to take command of the Eleventh Corps."

I had seen the General in Washington, and knew that he had lost one arm. "Please advance, General."

Oliver Otis Howard (1830 – 1909) was a career United States Army officer. He lost his right arm at Fair Oaks in June 1862 but returned to command. He played a major role at Gettysburg and after the Civil War commanded troops in the Indian Wars.—Ed. 2016

He rode forward alone, and being now sure that it was really he, I said:

"You may enter our lines," and then calmed the picket by calling out: "All right, Lieutenant, it's the Union General O. O. Howard, personally known to me."

As I escorted the General, he told me that General Siegel had requested to be relieved, and that he would take command of our corps. I indicated to him the shortest route to headquarters, and galloped away, halting at Schurz's headquarters to tell the news, and then at our headquarters. The Generals turned out to salute the new Commander and then made very long faces. It was a surprise to everybody. General Schurz had hoped to succeed General Siegel if the latter should resign, and my General would then have had a division.

Towards night the whole camp knew of the change in command, and after the first surprise, the feeling was bad enough. All the men had some affection for Siegel and had heard of the great show of piety of his successor, which had prejudiced them against him. Riding about at night, I heard various exclamations in the tents: "Boys, let us pray!" "Tracts now, instead of sauerkraut!" "Oh, Jesus!" "Oh, Lord!" Fortunately, all this excitement seemed to be good matured.

General Carl Schurz had many admirers as a great speaker, and was cheered whenever he dedicated a flag or talked on any subject. By reason of his superior mentality, personal bravery and sound judgment, he largely overcame his inexperience as a commanding officer.

Rumors now reached us that a Spring campaign was contemplated, and on the 25th of April, 1863, orders came for us to be ready to march at a moment's notice. Good bye, dear tent, beloved stove, and camp chair; farewell, comfort!

"We may be back," said my General. "It is better to leave everything as it is and I will place a guard in charge of our headquarters."

I had dreamed of entering Richmond, but the experienced General was not quite certain that we would reach there.

On April 27th we marched to Kelly's Ford and crossed the Rappahannock on the 28th in good style. The next day we were at Germanna Ford, and at night began to cross the Rapidan River. This fording of the river on a dark night, with just one headlight on the other shore offered the grandest sight I had yet enjoyed in the army. Not a word was spoken, and an awe-inspiring silence reigned. Regiment after regiment crossed the rapidly-flowing river, the men up to their hips in the water and holding their guns high above them. After I had crossed over on horseback I heard some faint screams. Thinking that an accident must have happened, I rode into the river again and found that a cook had fallen from an over-laden little mule and was nearly drowned. I told him to grasp Caesar's fine long tail and thus pulled him out; the mule, with many kettles to hamper him, had been washed down the river. I mention this because that cook, a Swiss boy, showed the greatest gratitude to me later on, and, after having secured some other kettles and a frying pan, he often brought me a good cup of coffee and once or twice some fancy fried crackers, covered with green herbs.

Silently the wet men followed us, now on a sandy road, through the woods, and we all expected to be welcomed at daybreak by shells from the enemy, but it seemed that our advance was so successfully made that General Lee, the great Commander of the Confederates, was not aware as yet that the

Army of the Potomac had crossed the two rivers. Some of our cavalry had had a fight with Southern cavalry in the woods the day before, but this was probably considered only an encounter of two reconnoitering parties.

CHAPTER III.

The Battle of Chancellorsville was a major battle war, fought from April 30 to May 6, 1863. Chancellorsville is often called as Robert E. Lee's "perfect battle" because his risky decision to divide his army in the presence of a much larger enemy force resulted in a significant Confederate victory. Despite winning the battle, Lee lost a greater percentage of his army and significantly lost General Stonewall Jackson. President Abraham Lincoln was quoted as saying, "My God! My God! What will the country say?"—Ed. 2016

On Friday afternoon, May 1, 1863, our First Brigade of the Third Division of the Eleventh Army Corps was placed in position parallel to a road and near the entrance of a plank road. We were facing south. Two of the regiments had woods before and behind them, one faced an open farm, and two stood north of us, in an open space surrounded by woods. General Scliimmelpfennig made his headquarters in an ambulance just north of the road, on the edge of the woods, and I prepared a place for myself to stretch out under the ambulance; naturally we were all terribly tired. But I was ordered to station the picket line first. I put Captain Steuernagel with his sharpshooters on the edge of a little triangle of woods where a wood road crossed the plank road, and Captain A. von Haake further south, this side of a small creek, with his outposts crossing the creek and on both sides of the wood road. I then galloped right and left to see if our outposts connected and reported that the necessary precautions had been taken. A few minutes later I fell into a sound sleep under the ambulance, with Caesar tied to a wheel and provided with some hay, which I had carried myself from a little farm near the road.

At daybreak, feeling well rested, I went to the farm and watered my horse, taking a good wash at the same time. Then I saddled Caesar carefully, woke the General and said: "With your permission I am off for a little reconnoitering trip."

"Go ahead," he replied, "but try to be back by eight."

I managed to get a cup of coffee from a company cook, lighted a cigar, and, in the best of spirits, rode in different directions while all the other officers and most of the men were still sleeping.

In the woods right before our outposts, I noticed an old negro. He slipped behind some trees, but I sternly ordered him to approach. The fellow seemed frightened, but I reassured him.

"Do you live 'round here, old man?" I asked.

"Yes, sail, fo' many years."

"Well, then, tell me all you know about this country. Where does this road lead?"

"Ole man Carpenter lived down there, but he's gone, sah, no one there now but two ole niggers."

"Come with me," I said, and he followed me to the open space north of us. "Where does, this plank road lead?"

"That's the way to Burton's ole place."

"How far to Burton?"

"Not a mile, marsa."

"Whose farm is that on the upper road?"

"Talley's, marsa, suah it is."

"And what is on the other side?"

"Why, marsa, there's the church, then Dowdall's tavern off yonder."

"How far?"

"I guess you'll ride it in eight minutes, marsa."

"To where does this plank road lead then?"

"If yo' go way up three miles or so, you'll see Chancellor's house, marsa, suah."

"What is beyond the church in the open ground?"

"Don't yo' see, marsa Hawkins's house yonder, that's Hawkins's, I'm suah, sah."

"All around these farms are woods?"

"Oh, Lawd, nothin' but woods and woods, marse. That there creek is Huntin' Run, and that there road goes to Ely's Ford, right through the woods, marsa. Oh, Lawd, how many soldiers!"

"And now, old man, speak the truth; where is General Lee and his army?"

"May Gawd curse me, marsa, if I don't tell the truth. Look there, don't yo' see Mars' Lee's men yonder; that's where they are."

And I could see plainly through my glasses, Confederates on a height south of us, probably a mile and three-quarters away.

"Is General Lee there himself?" I asked.

"The good Lawd knows, I reckon he's not far off. Jim told me—Jim's my son, marsa, and he's hidin' in the woods 'cause yo' see they took all the niggers away to work, Mars' Lee did—Jim says to me: 'Mars' Lee is not far!' He done thought that he was at Wolfort's, marsa,'way down yonder; of course yo' can't see it."

I dismounted, unfolded some paper, took a pencil, and telling the old nigger to sit next to me, made him repeat the names of the farms, roads and creeks; then I told him to go to the church and wait for me.

I galloped down to Burton's, up the plank road again to where it strikes the Pike road, west on the Pike past Dowdall's, east on the Pike to the 153rd Pennsylvania, through the woods to Colonel Gilsa, where I got some more coffee, back again to the church, north to Hawkins's farm, west to the batteries and back to the church, not far from which was Dilger's Battery, but he had ridden away. I sat down on the steps of the church and made a rough sketch with blue and red pencils, using a black one for the names. I had looked in vain for the old nigger, but after I had finished the sketch I noticed him talking to some of Captain Dilger's men and rode there, saying:

"Boys, keep the old nigger with you and when the Captain comes back, let him talk with him."

Leopold von Gilsa (1824 – 1870).

A little before eight that morning I saluted my General and sitting down by him I began to describe my sketch.

"We are here, General," I said, pointing to a blue spot. "As you know, in front of us, on the turnpike, lies in line of battle, the 68th Regiment, New York Volunteers, their left wing touches on the plank road. Next to the 68th comes the 61st Ohio, next to that the 74th Pennsylvania. In front of these regiments are small embankments, but the road is left clear and they are lying in the woods north of the Pike. Your two other regiments, the 82nd Illinois and the 157th New York, are posted north of us in close column, the first one near to the woods and the American Regiment almost in the middle of the open space. Both regiments are facing south.

"Next to your regiments along the Pike and west of us lies General Devens's Division, all the regiments in line of battle, facing south, except two of Colonel von Gilsa's Brigade, who are placed in the woods north of the Pike, facing west. These two regiments form the extreme right of our position. Our outpost line extends from east of the wood road, to past the plank road and connects with Steinwehr's and Devens's outposts. General Devens, commanding the Second Division, has his headquarters together with General McLean, who commands the brigade next to ours, at Talley's farm, close to the Pike. The 17th Connecticut, the 25th Ohio, the 107th Ohio, all American regiments, stand behind the open space fronting the farm. All the other regiments have woods in front: and in the rear. I found two of Captain Dike-man's guns on Talley's farm, facing south, besides some ambulances and wagons. Two of Dike-man's guns are with Gilsa's regiments, facing west, and two near the Pike road on the right, facing-south.

"Colonel Kryzanowsky, commanding the Second Brigade of Carl Schurz's Third Division of the Eleventh Corps, placed the 119th New York on a slight elevation east of the plank road, not far from where it strikes the Pike, and almost opposite the 68th New York. He

34

placed his other regiments on both sides of the road leading to Ely's Ford, north and south of Hawkins's farm, where General Carl Schurz has made his headquarters. These regiments stand in close column facing south, but one regiment is used for picket duty and its outposts are facing west in the woods. General Barlow,* commanding a Brigade of the First Division, is placed west of the Reserve Artillery, but I understand has orders to join General Steinwehr south of the plank road in front of Dowdall's Tavern, where General O. O. Howard has his headquarters. They told me that Steinwehr would soon march south to capture Lees rearguard.

The slight, boyish-looking Francis Channing Barlow (1834 –1896) was a lawyer, politician, and a incredibly fierce fighter.—Ed. 2016

"Near the church, and north of the Plank road, lies our safeguard, Captain Hubert Dilger's First Ohio Battery, supported by the 29th Regiment New York Volunteers. East of us, General, about two and a half miles from here, close to the Plank road, is Chancellor's farm. There are the headquarters of General Hooker, our army commander. I rode only far enough to notice a road that runs northeast from the Plank road, and on the other side straight south. A man at Dowdall's told me that it led to the so-called White House, northeast from here. Riding out past Dowdall's I could see no troops at all, and no corps seems to be near ours. Now, General, if you want to see some Confederate troops, take my glass and look down the wood road."

We walked a little south of the Pike, and the General had a long look at the enemy moving about in front of us.

"I think that we will advance soon," he said, "and I will be glad if we do, as, if they should come in on our flank we would be in a hell of a fix. Hallo, there comes Hooker down the road!"

We rushed to the Pike, and with the air of a king, holding his noble body very erect, approached the Commander of the Army of the Potomac. On his left I noticed General O. O. Howard, and behind these two Generals, several staff officers. Hooker and Howard hated each other, as is commonly known, and they did not hold much friendly conversation. We cheered, of course, but I disliked the conduct of the staff officers. Instead of looking carefully about and posting themselves, they fooled with each other and laughed aloud. Neither Hooker nor Howard saluted my General, but Hooker exchanged a few words with Devens. They soon rode back again towards Chancellor's, and the rumor was spread by Howard that Lee was running away from us. Soon after we received marching orders!

"Aha!" said my General. "We will have to chase after Lee, if he has really started to retreat." We were soon ready to commence the glorious pursuit, but the order to march was countermanded twenty minutes later, and we were ordered to keep quiet in our present positions. Until two that afternoon we lay about, resting, on this memorable second day of May. Then an aid brought the order from General Schurz to General Schimmelpfennig to send out, at once, a reconnoitering party of two or three companies south on the wood road, and to drive away or capture two guns which had just commenced to throw shells in our direction.

"Baron, take two companies of the 175th New York, let Captain Steuernagel join you with his sharpshooters. Deploy the men and march forward lively. You spy about and see what you can notice of Lee's movements."

We started down the wood road and deployed, soon reaching an open space again. The two guns fired, meantime, over our heads, and when we emerged again from the woods, they quickly took their departure, and disappeared in the woods opposite us. Just at that time, an aid of General Howard came chasing after us and gave the order to return to our old positions. I stopped near Captain von Haake's picket, sat down and talked to him. He said:

"I tell you, Baron, they will never come in this way. I have heard, the whole morning, the rolling of cannons on our right, and I believe the entire Confederate army is collecting at our flank. They are probably trying to surround us."

I reported this at once to General Schimmelpfennig.

"I have no doubt that Lee will come in on our flank," said the General. "You ride out carefully now, towards Burton's farm on the Plank road, and you, Captain Schleiter," (his Adjutant-General) "you trot to the right, and go as far as you can past Gilsa's position. Go ahead and find out all you can."

I changed horses and mounted my big bay, "Jim," now well rested; spurred him up and flew down the Plank road. Approaching Burton's farm, I went at a slow trot, with my eyes wide open, halted about sixty yards from there, and got my spy glasses out. All at once a shot was fired and hit Jim in the upper hind leg, the blood pouring out profusely; I perceived at once some twenty-five cavalrymen, led by an officer on a small gray horse, emerging from behind Burton's house. I wheeled my horse around, and spurring and whipping him with my sword, galloped away towards our lines.

"Surrender! Surrender!" they halloed after me, firing at the same time. I drew my revolver and fired backwards, urging my horse to his utmost speed on that rough plank road. Several times he nearly fell, but soon I came in sight of Captain Steuernagel's men, the Confederates coming closer and closer behind me. I was bending forward almost level with my saddle, and was enveloped in a cloud of dust, when I heard distinctly the command:

"Wait, boys, wait; now, ready, aim—fire!"

"Help, Marie!" I screamed. Some forty bullets came whizzing towards me, and my horse fell like a log, pierced by many balls. I pitched head first to the ground, when another volley, over my head, made the Confederates turn about and gallop off.

When the smoke and dust had blown away, Captain Steuernagel and some men approached me and said: "Too bad we had to fire at you, but we thought it was a Confederate attack."

They helped me up, and I ached from head to foot. I had fallen on the saddle-knob with great force and felt very faint.

"See where I am wounded" I said. They examined me all over; no blood except on the left cheek, and someone pulled out a splinter, but one of my high boots was pierced, my spy glass was demolished, my scabbard bent in two places, and the horse was dead. He had been bleeding from some half dozen wounds. They rubbed the dirt off my clothes, and I exclaimed more than once: "That was a lucky escape; thanks, Marie!" I begged one of the men to assist me to find the nearest surgeon, as I was suffering tremendous pain. He took me to Surgeon Reissberg, and I had to undergo a painful operation, but he relieved me a great deal, and soon I was able to walk towards my General.

"The first shots have been fired," I said, "and unfortunately, my good bay horse received them," and I reported the circumstances. Just then Captain Schleiter arrived, and in a very excited way reported that the Confederates were massing on our right,

"I rode out some hundred yards west of Colonel Gilsa's outposts," he said, "and distinctly heard commands given by Confederate officers. I am sure that they will come in on the Pike, and all-the regiments are facing south."

The General called at once for his horse and rode away to speak to Schurz, who was at Howard's headquarters. The General would not go there, but sent full reports by one of Schurz's staff officers. This must have been about three-forty in the afternoon. My servant had taken the saddle and bridle off the dead horse by this time, and I purchased a United States horse at the ambulance corps for one hundred and twenty-five dollars, which he mounted, while I held noble Caesar again by the bridle.

Five o'clock and no changes! The regiments remained facing south on the Pike, and only two regiments, north of us, were ordered to face west. Still my General had spoken to the different commanders of the regiments, and told them that if an attack should be made from the flank they should fall back to the edge of the woods, at the cross road, and, if pressed hard, to near the church and get behind Captain Dilger's Battery. The 68th New [York, the 61st Ohio and the 74th Pennsylvania were to wheel in line with the 82d Illinois and the 157th New York.

The well-rested troops had begun making coffee and preparing meals about four o'clock. Arms were stacked all along the Pike, and not one of us expected an attack before May 3d, in the morning. All of us believing that if Lee intended to attack our flank it would take him all night to form his regiments, as we still saw Confederates in front of us. All the Colonels with whom I spoke shared my opinion that an attack would be made from the flank, except Colonel Hecker of the 82d Illinois. When I mentioned my fears to him, he flew into a passion, and said very roughly:

"*Alles Dummheit*! They are not fools enough to attack us through these dense woods." But the other Colonels could not understand why Howard did not change his front and make some preparations for the safety of his corps. Of course, I expected that he had at least some cavalry, or competent staff officers out to watch the movements of the enemy, as I was hearing again and again that Howard knew that Lee was fast retreating. I tried to persuade myself that this might be true, and after a time I firmly believed, once more, that we would be attacked the next morning. Could I have guessed the horrible disgrace my good corps would have to endure later on, I would have ridden up to General Howard's headquarters and would have implored him for better protection of our flank. Actually, now and then, such a resolution induced me to mount my horse, but then I said to myself: "They must know better! What can an aid-de-camp of a brigade know about the precautions of a corps commander!"

CHAPTER IV.

About five o'clock I called my servant, Frankel, and said: "I'll take care of Caesar to-night, and you camp near the other two horses, but get some oats if you can."

"None to be had, sir. I rode all about to get some feed."

"Ride over to General Howard's headquarters," I continued, "and beg some oats, or if necessary, give some fellow a dollar and make him furnish you oats enough for Caesar, at least, as I hate to see the dear fellow starve."

So Frankel mounted my new horse, and leading the iron-grey pack horse, rode towards Dowdall's Tavern—a lucky move for him and for me! At about half past five I mounted Caesar and rode to the 61st Ohio, where I had a chat with Colonel McGroarty.

All at once I heard some noise. I listened, and down the Pike came a cannon ball, ricocheting; then I heard firing in the woods, and some queer sounds. I galloped to the ambulance, where my General was resting, loosened his horse and said:

"They are coming, General, and right through the woods on our flank." He mounted, rode to the Cross road, and excitedly gave the order to tell the commanders of his regiments on the Pike to change front and to form in line of battle north of the Plank road, a little east of the Cross road.

I delivered these orders safely and promptly, but as the men had been informed that Lee was running away, they had taken things easy, were lying about in groups and smoking pipes, or were looking for the best places to sleep in peace and comfort that night.

The command "Fall in," and the firing in the woods now naturally created the greatest commotion. Men began fighting for their guns, stacks of arms were upset everywhere, many trying to repack their knapsacks and roll up their blankets, pushing one another, trying to fix their accoutrements, while the excited shouts of the officers: "Fall in! fall in!" caused much disorder.

40

So it took some time before all the men fell in line and until the regiments were ready to march away to the new positions. General Devens's men already came running down the road, thoroughly demoralized and panic stricken.

General Devens had not done a thing to prevent the great disaster, and with no other excuse except that General Howard had approved his position in the morning. Now his poor men came running down the Pike, shouting such warnings as: "We are all surrounded!" "Keep off the road, boys; the Confederates have just placed a battery on it, and will fire away," etc.

Behind the first rush of the frantic and disgusted men, attacked in the flank and partially the rear, and surprised in broad daylight, came rattling down two of Dieckman's guns. There was only one driver to direct the course of the first gun, and the leaders, without a driver—seeing the road blocked, and as some men, unable to get out of the way, were shouting at them—turned from the road into Talley's farm, smashing things generally till the gun got stuck, and the horses fell down.

Greater and greater became the rush, shells came flying down the road, the two guns, formerly stationed at the farm, hitched up, and were trying to get on the road, but were prevented by the bayonets of Devens's desperate men. They then dashed into the woods of the little triangle mentioned before, just when Captain Steuernagel and Captain von Haake led their men north to rejoin the 68th New York, as no enemy had advanced towards their picket line and they had observed the attack from their rear. These two guns were abandoned and the cannoniers and drivers came in with our outposts.

Our regiments on the Pike were blocked in and could not move, and already the bullets from the Confederates came whizzing into the ranks. General Schimmelpfennig shouted: "First Brigade, form here!"

"Form here, men of the First Brigade!" I sang out continually.

The officers of these regiments tried hard to lead the men there, fighting their way through Devens's panic-stricken men, but the confusion was too great. At that time General Howard arrived at a

41

point about forty paces west of the Cross road, fell or jumped from his horse, and screamed: "Stand, boys, face about and fire!"

All very nice, but naturally without the slightest effect! I had caught his horse and called out to him to mount.

"No, take that horse to the rear!" he shouted.

"Can't do that, General," I said, "and you'd better mount, sir, as the Confederates are quite near!"

Hundreds were killed near us that moment. As he did not seem to be able to get on his horse I dismounted, grasped the back of his coat and helped him on. Than he rode towards Dowdall's.

I now worked my way to General Schimmelpfennig, and he sang out to me "Bring the 82nd Illinois near this cross road and place it next to the 68th."

I brought the 82nd in double quick, down towards the General, when he gave the order:

"Too late, too late! Let Hecker front west at his old position, and I will collect the other men right behind him!"

"*Verflugter Esel!*" roared Colonel Hecker and then gave the command: "About face! Double quick! March!"

I rode along and waited till he commanded:

"Halt—Front—Fire!" The Confederates were already visible in the woods before him. Deer, rabbits and foxes came racing out of the woods. Just then Hecker's color bearer was killed, and the old Revolutionist seized the flag, and shouted: "Fix bayonets! Charge bayonets! Come on, boys! Charge!"

He was going to take the woods by storm, but that moment a bullet struck him, and he fell from his horse, screaming: "Fire away, 82nd!" and they did fire away nobly, and remained at their post. I now noticed my General right in the rear of this brave regiment, forming the men, and I assisted to get as many as I could in line. Devens's men had all passed up the Plank road, and were running towards Chancellor's. The 68th New York held its place well on the

Cross road, the 61st joined it partially, but our other men mostly ran behind the 82nd, and were with the General.

I galloped about, and was just going to tell the Commander of the 68th to fall back behind the 82nd also, in order to allow Captain Dilger to fire down the road—he was sending shells over their heads—when "Pfutt!" a bullet struck me in the belt plate, and nearly threw me off Caesar's back. Holding myself by his mane, I got into the saddle again, but thinking that I was mortally wounded, as I felt the pain in my back, and naturally thought that the bullet had pierced my stomach, I turned east, and chased toward Dowdall's to die away from the great tumult.

Just in front of Dowdall's I noticed General Howard holding a flag under his arm and shouting: "Rally round the flag; rally round the flag!" Mechanically I drew my sword and stopped some men coming up the road, but my voice gave out and I felt a new and fearful pain in my stomach. Thinking that my hour had come, I walked Caesar past Howard, and with eyes directed toward heaven, said: "I am coming, Marie, make my sufferings short!"

But soon the pain grew a little lighter again and noticing Howard galloping to the rear, and Schurz and several other mounted officers also working their way toward Chancellor's, followed by all the men, I took a last look at the front.

Heroic Captain Dilger, who had his battery across the Plank road, stuck to his position, and seeing now nothing but Confederates before him, commenced firing canister and grape shot in every direction. Our men, who had held themselves bravely west of the church, had been compelled—attacked as they were by overwhelming forces—to retire and some had gathered in the rear of Captain Dilger's battery. I would have liked to take command of these brave fellows, but felt more and more hors-de-combat. Strange, sharp pains in my stomach troubled me, my head was swimming and Caesar, as if conscious of this, all at once reared and tore up the Plank road behind the different generals. I observed a battery on the right of the road, and turned Caesar towards it. He stopped near the other horses, and I fainted and fell from his back.

How long I lay there I do not know, but when I opened my eyes again it was dark. I asked a man: "Where am I?"

"Behind Captain Best's Battery."

"Is Captain Hubert Dilger here?"

"No, but four of his guns are with us; he has been firing with one gun on the road, retreating only from time to time far enough not to have it captured, but I hear no more shots and he may be here soon, if he is still alive."

"God grant that he is," I sighed. "When he comes, tell him that I am here and want to shake hands with him before I die."

"Are you badly wounded?" asked a lieutenant.

"The bullet struck me here," I answered, pointing to the belt plate.

"That is a bad place; let me send you in an ambulance to the surgeon at Chancellor's."

I thanked him, an ambulance came, they lifted me in and drove me at full speed to a place behind Chancellor's. A surgeon cut open the belt, as it would not unhook, opened my garments and showing me a round bullet, said:

"You are a lucky fellow; the bullet struck the heavy belt-plate, bent it way in, then the ball passed through the leather and the clothing and lodged itself on your stomach, making only a deep impression and coloring your whole body in rainbow tints." He put plasters crosswise over the wound and said: "I think that you will be all right; in a day or two you may be able to ride again."

This was a pleasant surprise, and after the surgeon had kindly given me brandy, I asked the ambulance man to drive me back to where he had picked me up. I climbed out, feeling very shaky on my legs, and to my delight, was soon greeted by Captain Dilger. My voice had given out, but I could whisper to him to let someone hunt up Caesar; then he enlightened me about the last part of the fight on that dreadful day.

"It was Jackson who attacked us," he said, "and he drove us all the way up to here. Some of our troops have taken a stand below this hill, but the fight is over for today, I believe. Still we are ready if they want to make a night charge. This is Fair-view, and we have nearly fifty guns in line."

"We were badly beaten," I whispered.

"What else could you expect?" he answered. "Why, Napoleon's Guard could not have held itself better, in such dreadful circumstances. God knows that I reported Jackson's movements in time, but I was insulted by some impudent major at Hooker's headquarters when I reported that they were massing on our flank, and then just see how they placed us—without any reserves!"

"I wonder where my General is?" I asked.

"He cannot be far off, unless he rode up the road toward the White House. His men held out as long as they could; the regiments on the Cross road ran through the woods in front of here, and those that made a stand near Hawkins's farm probably retired towards the White House, while I was banging away on the Plank road. One company of the Gist Ohio, and some men of the 68th New York, stuck to me bravely and the Confederates often got so close to my guns that the boys had to do a good deal of firing. I was nearly captured myself, but a brave young fellow brought a horse to me after mine was shot."

Just then a man approached, leading Caesar, and asked if that was my horse.

"Yes, it is, a thousand thanks," I said gratefully. "Help me on to him, as I have to hunt up General Schimmelpfennig."

"You lie quiet," said Dilger, sternly, and after ordering his man to keep my horse with the Battery horses, he asked me if I was hungry. As I did not answer, he brought me two crackers with some devilled ham on them and, in spite of the fearful contusion my stomach had received, I ate a little.

"You can't find Schimmelpfennig to-night," he said. "Lie on this blanket and sleep, so that you will feel strong enough to fight tomorrow."

I crawled toward a big stone, covered it with part of the blanket, laid my aching head on it and closed my eyes. The attack, the ambulance, the surgeon, all my surroundings faded away and Marie alone was near me, her big, soft eyes shining with protection and love.

When I awoke, a cannonier informed me that it was nearly three in the morning. "Please help me up, I am stiff as a log."

I regained my feet with great trouble, but after moving my muscles about and drinking a cup of hot coffee, I was able to mount Caesar. Meeting a sergeant of the 68th New York, he told me that what was left of the regiment lay about the field near Chancellor's and that a mounted officer had just called out:

"The Eleventh Corps to rally near the road east of Chancellor's."

I told him to walk next to me and sing out this order. He did so with a wonderfully strong voice and soon some men of the unfortunate corps came strolling our way. By six o'clock I had about five hundred men of our Brigade around me, all looking tired and sad. An hour later General Schimmelpfennig arrived and we now tried to form regiments, I perceiving with some satisfaction that all our flags were safe.

When Frankel reported with my two other horses I repaired with him behind some trees and let him clean me up a little.

"I have some oats," he said, "and if you dismount, sir, I will give Caesar a good breakfast. The other two horses had all they could eat during the night, as I was lucky enough to capture this sack at Chancellor's the moment I had arrived."

"How long have you been here?" I asked.

"Oh, since before dark. When the fuss began, I galloped way back here to save your horses."

After dismounting, I walked back to the Brigade and soon an officer brought the order: "The Eleventh Corps will march to the extreme left, and occupy the strong works thrown up by Humphrey's Division."

Without waiting for other organization, my General rode in that direction, followed by all the present members of his Brigade and some of our men who had joined the forces below the batteries reached us only late in the afternoon.

We found the ditches behind the breastworks full of water, as it had rained hard in that neighborhood. Most of the men took off their shoes and had

A a good foot bath, following the example of Colonel McGroarty of the bloody Irish 61st Ohio, wounded according to his often repeated statements twenty-nine times in former actions, but coming through this one without a scratch.

The General took up his position behind some tremendous trees, and seemed to be in a very bad humor. After scolding Captain Schleiter for not knowing yet about the ammunition on hand, he said to me:

"Where, were you, Baron, after I left the Cross road?"

"I brought the 82nd Illinois back to its original position, then helped you to collect the men, rode over to get the 68th towards you, and to stop some men of the 61st, but got shot in the belt-plate which nearly threw me from my horse. This shot, which I thought more serious than it really was, and the consequences of my fall, when Jim was killed under me in the afternoon, made me unfit for duty and after stopping at Dowdall's and seeing you gallop to the rear, I rode behind Captain Best's Battery."

"Go out, please, and see if we connect with other troops," he resumed.

"Would it not be better to place a skirmish line in front of the breastworks, sir?" I asked.

He answered furiously, "No!"

I mounted my United States horse and rode away. I had been exposed scarcely two minutes when four or five shots were fired at me from the woods in front of the rifle-pits, and one ball grazed my cap. I halted and asked Colonel McGroarty what this could mean.

47

"We got them in front this time," he answered. "As soon as a man peeps over the rifle-pits a bullet comes flying."

I rode on and found that our Brigade was on the extreme left, and in line with the other Brigades of the Eleventh Corps, and heard that the Corps lacked two thousand five hundred men. I met one of General Howard's staff officers and asked what Corps was next to ours.

"General Couch's," I was told.

"Any reserves behind us?"

"I don't know."

I rode on, found a gap next to the Eleventh, and then other troops behind rifle-pits.

"What Corps is this?" I questioned.

"General Meade's," was the answer.

"They told me General Couch's."

"No, he is on the other side of Chancellor's House."

I hunted up the nearest colonel and said: "There is a gap between your corps and ours. Please report it and see that it is filled."

"We are comfortable enough here, fill it with runaway Dutchmen," the brute replied. We poor German-Americans were frequently alluded to by Know-Nothings* as "Dutchmen," and I was determined to rescind this "nickname" on all occasions.

*The Know Nothings were an organized nativist movement opposed to immigration. The Germans in particular came in for lots of abuse from this group.—Ed. 2016

"I will not stand this!" I said furiously. "I am no more of a Dutchman than you are. I am a German officer who offered his sword to assist in this great war in order to earn the noble title of an American citizen and to keep the great Union together." Then I uttered an oath and galloped away.

That gap remained for twenty-four hours, although I sent notice to headquarters by some Lieutenant, who acted as an aid-de-camp to the General.

Just as I returned to meet Schimmelpfennig, six or seven shots were fired at me again and my poor horse got a bullet through the root of his tail, and another ball tore the heel of my right boot away—another wonderful escape, as the heel of my foot did not even bleed. I then listened to the new order of General Schimmelpfennig:

"You should find out," he said, "whether we have a skirmish line in front, or only bushwhackers; you'd better go out with some volunteers."

I tied my horse, walked to the regiments and sang out in a low voice: "A few volunteers to accompany me outside the line to find out where those shots come from."

Eight officers of the German regiments advanced at once, took guns from their men and we jumped over the rifle-pits. I gave the command:

"Deploy as skirmishers, double quick, march! Forward march!" and we penetrated into the woods. Only one shot was fired at us which wounded a lieutenant. Then we saw some men running away and fired at them. After going forward about six hundred yards we wounded a man whom we perceived behind us, and who probably had lain concealed when we passed. I ran towards him and asked to what corps he belonged.

"None, we are farmers, but are ordered to annoy you damned Yanks!"

So we now knew that no army confronted us; we bandaged the outlaw, who had a bullet through his leg, and assisted him towards our lines. When about one hundred yards from the rifle-pits, the bush-whackers, who had again followed us up, fired five or six shots, which passed over our heads and struck near General Schimmelpfennig's tree. He thought that this was the beginning of an attack, and gave the signal:

"Brigade, fire!"

One of my volunteers screamed: "Lie down—that signal means: 'Brigade, fire!'"

And a moment later hundreds of shots whistled over our heads, into the woods.

After three salvos, the signal: "Cease firing," was given. We got up carefully and ran to the rifle-pits, calling out:

"Don't fire, we belong to your Brigade!"

We climbed inside, the men cheering us lustily, and assuming a very cool air to hide oy indignation, I reported to the General:

"Only bushwhackers, sir, are in front; thanks for driving them away."

"My God, were you still out?" he exclaimed.

"Yes, sir, I was, with a few brave fellows besides!"

"That is too bad, I imagined that you had returned," he said.

"A funny mistake," I rejoined, "but fortunately none of us were killed thereby. Here comes a captured bushwhacker."

CHAPTER V.

Our men wanted to shoot or hang the bushwhacker, but the General had him brought to General Howard's headquarters, and I never heard anything more of him. No notice was taken of my gallant band. The firing of the Brigade had fortunately driven the bush-whackers away and there were no more bullets from that direction.

Night came, and Frankel made as good a bed as he could for me. Caesar, after enjoying the last oats in the sack, lay down next to me, impolitely but very appropriately turning his back, and I excused him as I felt much safer, knowing that in case he should dream and gesticulate with his legs, his hoofs would not strike me. I could not sleep, and I lay there tossing about until I became so nervous that I called Frankel and said:

"Just to quiet my nerves, look for the positively last cigar."

He found one in the side pocket of my best jacket, after unpacking everything loaded on the packsaddle. I smoked with delight, although my supper had consisted only of two crackers and some tea boiled with very dirty water. "God bless you, Saint Manitou, you who gave the first tobacco for the solace of mankind!" I exclaimed.

The annoying experiences of the day occupied my mind, but after getting alternately mad and disgusted, I concluded that I had been most lucky in escaping the bullets of friends and foes, and my thoughts naturally turned to my Protecting Angel. I thanked her with all my heart for her fostering care, and saying: "Good-night, Marie," I fell asleep at last.

At day-break I nose and made a most elaborate toilet, changing my underclothing and my suit, and was much refreshed. Frankel, that king of valets and grooms, having everything handy, I even shaved, as I honestly believe in the outward appearance of an officer, even on the battlefield. A general dressed in a sutler's coat and sitting on a horse equipped like that of a common cavalry man does not greatly inspire the soldiers.

I then had a cup of coffee and walked about to see how the men felt.

"We are all out of rations, sir," they complained to me. "Not a cracker is left and no coffee."

I promised to see what could be done, and when the General opened his eyes for the first time, I reported their wants.

"Ride over to Schurz and find out if rations are coming," he said.

There they could not understand why supplies had not reached us during the night, as loaded mules were expected from the Rappahannock River. I galloped Caesar a few miles in that direction, and met a sutler wagon. On inquiring, the Jew told me that green mules had been loaded with crackers, but that they had kicked and rolled over and would not go.

"Where are you bound?" I asked.

"To the First Corps."

"You can't reach them. They are too far away and probably engaged now as I hear the roar of cannons. You'd better come to the Eleventh and sell out; we need a bite."

"Can't do it!" he said roughly.

"Can't! Well, let us try some persuasion; you drive after me or I'll blow your brains out!" saying this I pulled my revolvers, and for the first time in my life, played the part of a highway robber, looking very savage all the while, but laughing to myself, as I had not the slightest intention of hurting the poor devil.

Scared to death, he followed me, and when we reached the Brigade I said: "Boys, here are eatables and delicacies. Let the first sergeants take down the amount of things the men purchase and we will collect it next pay-day and hand it over to this kind individual."

A lively sale commenced, and I had trouble in securing a couple of boxes of cigars, some canned goods, cakes, sausages, etc., for my headquarters, but to set a good example, I paid the sutler cash, calling out to the men:

"All pay who can; the balance may have credit till next pay-day."

In one hour the wagon was empty, and the sales had been made in pretty decent style. When I came back I saw some paying cash and the sergeants gave the sutler a copy of the names of his new debtors. Then I ordered the fellow off and told him to hurry to the river on he would soon smell powder. To my great satisfaction, he drove away at a lively rate, but not until he had my name carefully noted down.

"I will hold you responsible for every cent," he said.

All was joy now! Coffee, sugar, sausages, cakes, cigars! In a short time we felt like heroes, and 'it was a pity that Jackson's men did not attack us—and for a change, from the front. But everything remained quiet.

I went out reconnoitering a couple of times, and when a squad of men under Captain Spraul, of General Schurz's staff refused to enter the woods in front of Schurz's headquarters, whence some shots occasionally came flying, I rode all alone on the top of the hill through the woods and reported: "Only bush-whackers again!"

Gallant Captain Dilger, who was always at Schurz's headquarters, said to me: "Don't do such things, Baron, you risk your life for nothing, and you will never get credit for it; these fellows here call it foolhardiness, and you only make them jealous by trying to distinguish yourself."

"That may be so, dear friend," I replied, "but I can't act cowardly—it is not in me, and maybe someday old comrades will honor me for my bravery and the nation show me some gratitude. Don't you think, Dilger, that foreign-born soldiers, who believe in the institutions of this country, who have offered their services to save this glorious Union and to abolish slavery, who stand these tremendous hardships—march thirty and forty miles on bad roads in the wilderness, trying to keep their souls and bodies together by swallowing hardtack and dirty bacon—and who are willing to fight and die for their adopted Fatherland, are as much Americans as soldiers born in this country? Do you not think they are more entitled to be called Americans than all those natives who have remained at home and become rich, while we are serving for

53

greenbacks worth thirty-five cents on the dollar; serving in fact for nothing, since the pay hardly enables us to buy the necessities of life."

"You are right, Baron," he answered, "but, as I told you, it will do you no good to try to distinguish yourself—you will only be killed and buried unknown, as your rank is not high enough and promotion impossible."

It has always been a principle of mine never to care much what others thought about me, but to let my own conscience, the God in me, criticize my actions. Somehow or other though, Captain Dilger's remark made an impression and I said to myself:

"Keep your ambition down, old fellow; you are not among friends, and no one takes the slightest interest in you. Spare the horseflesh, do only what the General orders you, and do it well in order to satisfy your own conscience."

The terrible defeat of the first day of the battle weighed heavily on me; I knew that I had done my duty thoroughly and conscientiously, but the Eleventh Corps undoubtedly ran, and although fully excusable for doing so, I knew it would none the less be blamed. I became actually melancholy, sat down within speaking distance of my General, smoked the newly purchased cigars, and was lost in gloomy meditation. Even my thoughts of Marie could hardly soothe my troubled mind.

On the sixth of May orders came for the Eleventh Corps to march to United States Ford to recross the Rappahannock River on pontoon bridges, protected by thirty-two guns, and to march back to the old camps.

I recrossed with a heavy heart, and after a talk with General Schurz I felt tears rolling down my cheeks. I was ashamed of this battle, and deplored the sad experience of the Eleventh Corps.

Reaching camp I found my tent, with all the old comforts, and after attending to my picket and outpost duties, I was more or less at leisure. I wrote in my daybook, and was ready to assist the General in his report. The latter did not leave his tent for a week; most of the time he was in bed, and very cross when the Adjutant-General reported or asked for orders. His orderly told me that the General seemed to be sick, and so one day I scratched at the tent and entered.

"The picket line is the same as before, General," I reported. "I inspect it every day and night."

No answer.

"I am afraid that you are sick, General; can I do anything for you?"

"No."

"When you are ready to make your report, sir, I have drawn some plans of our positions."

No answer.

"Have you read the *Herald*, sir? They state that the German troops behaved in a most cowardly manner. That we were the cause of the late disaster."

General Howard reportedly blamed the German troops for his own mistakes.—Ed. 2016

"Just what I expected," he said. "Am I mentioned?"

"No, sir; but General Schurz is, and often, too."

"Bring me all the papers to-morrow," he said. "I have a headache now."

I stepped out, collected all the articles against us out of the papers, from May third to date, pinned them together and left them, the next morning, on the General's desk, near the entrance to his tent. My tent was near his, and soon I heard him reading aloud the defaming paragraphs, then swearing like an old trooper. He called for his horse, rode to Schurz's headquarters, and then proceeded to General Howard.

At night he called us to his tent and addressed us. It was an astonishingly good oratorical effort, and ended in a scorching denunciation of the press. Then he ordered us to hand him, by the next day, reports of the different regimental commanders and an account of our own experiences. I wrote mine, personally, as above.

After perusing the reports of the colonels he sat down and wrote his report, which took him the entire night, and after handing it to me to forward he went for a ride. He had used only my maps.

Later on it has been emphatically stated over and over again that no corps in the Army, surprised and surrounded as the Eleventh Corps was at Chancellorsville, could have held its ground better under similar circumstances.

The Major of the 68th had been killed at Chancellorsville, several captains had resigned, and I now saw a chance for promotion. I applied and received, on May 29th, a commission as Captain of Company A, 68th New York, from Governor Seymour, and was mustered into the United States service as such June 17, 1863.

I carefully inspected my company, took stock of the accoutrements, tents, etc., made an encouraging address to the boys, sent in my report, treated the company to beer and eatables, and then turned the very small company over to the First Lieutenant and remained on Schimmelpfennig's stall.

During the weeks following we had a parade before President Lincoln, and arranged races between the officers. I won the first prize on my fleet Caesar. He alone jumped a five-foot fence, with a nine-foot wide ditch behind it. Most of the other officers fell into the ditch; even Prince Salm-Salm,* a celebrated rider, who was Colonel of the 8th New York. President Lincoln handed me a beautiful riding whip as a tribute to my horsemanship, but he did not recognize in me the man who had been especially recommended to him in 1862.

Prince Salm-Salm met and married an American woman. She followed him throughout his service in the war. Her memoir is An American Princess in the Civil War.—Ed. 2016

As very little friendship was extended to me in our Brigade Headquarters I became a frequent visitor to Colonel von Gilsa and General von Steinwehr, both fine officers and thorough gentlemen. Emil Frey,* at that time a Captain in the 82d Illinois, became one of my dearest friends, as he had been educated at the same college with my brother, and knew my family well.

Emil Johann Rudolf Frey (1838 –1922) was a Swiss politician who immigrated to America in 1848.—Ed. 2016

On June 8th we received marching orders.

On the 13th we reached Catlett's Station, and from what I could hear we belonged to the left wing of the army, and were under command of General Reynolds, who was placed over the commanders of the First, Third and Eleventh Corps. General Howard commanded the Eleventh, General Francis C. Barlow the First Division, and Colonel Leopold von Gilsa the First Brigade of that Division.

The 68th New York had been transferred from Schimmelpfennig's Brigade to Colonel von Gilsa's, and when at Catlett's Station, the latter claimed my services on his staff. As General S. observed that I could do as I liked I preferred the change, for I was now on much more friendly terms with Colonel von Gilsa than with my present General, who was cross with all the officers, and hardly ever disposed to talk or give any information.

The First Brigade consisted of the 68th New York, the 41st New York, the 54th New York, and the 153d Pennsylvania. I knew all the Commanders, and was received with politeness when I reported. Brigadier General Adelbert Ames commanded the Second Brigade of our division, and I became acquainted with this magnificent, brave and handsome Commander on the next day's march.

On June 15th the First, Sixth and Eleventh Corps were grouped around Centreville. We heard men talk of Lee's invasion of the North, and learned that General Hooker was moving parallel to Lee's line of advance. "May we meet Lee somewhere soon," I said to Colonel von Gilsa, "and may the Eleventh Corps prove that it is as good and brave as any other, small as it is now."

On June 22d we were stationed on Goose Creek, and we all turned into washerwomen. To the horror of Frankel, who was washing and rubbing away on a flat stone, I tried to supply myself with clean handkerchiefs, and stood half undressed in the middle of the creek, dipping half a dozen in and out. We had a great time, and felt much refreshed towards night.

On the 28th we marched through Boonsboro and, after placing the outposts as usual, I rode up to the Corps headquarters to get some news.

"General Hooker has resigned," Major Howard told me in a subdued voice, "and General George S. [sic] Meade has been assigned to the command of the Army of the Potomac."

George Gordon Meade wrote to his wife that when he was awakened in his tent, he assumed army politics had caught up to him and he was going to be arrested. Instead, he was given command of the army—only two days before the Battle of Gettysburg. See The Life and Letters of George Gordon Meade, Volume II.—Ed. 2016

"And why?" I asked. "We all like Hooker, in spite of Chancellorsville."

"General Halleck worked against him," explained the Major, "and he got disgusted with the interference at Washington."

Next morning we tramped on again and camped at night on a slight elevation. The troops were very tired, and while I was sitting with Colonel von Gilsa and several officers, waiting for the coffee to boil, a Sergeant came and placed a big iron pail before us, saying:

"With the compliments of the Commissary."

I smelled the contents and reported: "Whiskey."

"Let us taste it," said the Colonel, and each of us dipped his tin cup in; without intention, mine was filled to the brim.

"Here's to our new commander, General Meade," said the Colonel, and we all took a drink. The Colonel, noticing that I had only tasted mine, said: "That won't do; drain your cup to such a toast as this!" And foolishly I swallowed the entire contents. Soon the blood mounted to my head, and I began to feel quite dizzy. The Commissary arrived a few minutes after we had drunk the toast, and complained to the Colonel that he had some fresh meat in the valley below, and that the boys refused to get it on the plea of being too tired.

"Please order them down, sir, as I must be off," he added.

"I'll make them go," I said, and walking through the camps I waved a stick I had picked up and sang out: "Go for meat, boys, and quickly, too." Then feeling that my steps were becoming uncertain, and noticing Frankel behind me, I exclaimed:

"Frankel, hold tight!" He grasped my jacket and kept me steady, and the boys laughed as they ran down the hill.

On the march, to Emmetsburg, where we arrived on the thirtieth, I was trotting by the Brigade, and to my horror the drummer boys of the 68th cried out loudly:

"Frankel!" And all the regiments answered:

"Hold tight!"

This joke followed me through all the marches, but it always revived the spirits of the men, who invariably laughed at it, even though they grumbled and cursed through the tedious marches. This induced me never to stop it, but rather to encourage it with a smile.

As this was the only time that I imbibed liquor freely during the war, and as I was always seen perfectly sober, it could not hurt my reputation still the joke spread, and sometimes I felt annoyed when it was mentioned by higher officers, and I would no doubt have lost the good will of General Howard [a devout Christian] by it if he had chanced to know that Baron von Fritsch was an aid-de-camp, and that he had helped him to mount his horse on the Cross road at the battle of Chancellorsville, most probably saving his life by doing so.

On July 1st, at dawn, we were awakened and at once began preparations to march, but not until about eight that morning did our Division follow closely the First Corps towards Gettysburg. About eleven we were ordered to proceed on the double quick, and we heard the roaring of cannons at a distance.

Colonel von Gilsa was under arrest for having allowed more than one man at a time to leave the ranks to fetch water, and I galloped forward to General Barlow, a very strict commander, and praising the gallantry of my Colonel asked him to allow me to return his sword.

"You can do so, under the circumstances, but keep your men well together. Staff officers may even shoot down stragglers, and I demand the strictest discipline."

I returned the sword, and mounting my good charger, Caesar, I asked permission to ride ahead and see what our chances were for glory. I chased up the Emmetsburg road, and entered Gettysburg just as General Howard came out of a building, from the roof of which he had been surveying the neighborhood.

I reported the Eleventh Corps only a mile away, asked a citizen to hold Caesar, and climbed to the top of the same building, accompanied by a smart, young boy, who knew the neighborhood. I noticed large troops of cavalry on the left of the town, saw cannons firing on a hill close to Gettysburg, located the Baltimore Railway on the west, and the guns of the First Corps answering from the heights, where the Lutheran Seminary was located.

Rushing down again, I heard that General [John] Reynolds had been killed, and that General Howard claimed the command of the left wing.

At full speed I returned to our Corps and brought the latest news to the Generals, and Carl Schurz galloped to the front, at last a Corps Commander.

We marched right through Gettysburg, and to the right, over an open field, towards the Harrisburg road, where we were heavily bombarded. Large shells and six-pounders passed close over our heads, many officers dismounted or bent low whenever they felt the pressure of the air created by the shot.

Gilsa's Brigade took an apparently fine position on a wooded knoll this side of Rock Creek, and General Ames's Brigade was stationed just outside of it, as a reserve. It proved to be a hot place for us. Trees were felled everywhere by the cannon balls, and one unfortunate officer was nailed by a six-pounder against a big tree. I

60

got hold of his bushy hair and pulled him down, as he presented a ghastly appearance.

Our men were first ordered to sit down, and we mounted officers gathered around General Barlow, the Division Commander, outside the woods.

"Take a skirmish line out in front of us, Baron," he said to me, "and stretch the men to the right."

I deployed a company, and by two o'clock the Confederate skirmish line faced us, and firing began at once. I rode up and down, encouraging the men to keep cool and aim well, and soon we drove the Confederate skirmishers back.

But now I noticed heavy columns approaching in front, and from the right. We fired, and then I ordered the commanding officer of the skirmishers to fall slowly back into the woods and fire from tree to tree. Then I rode to the Brigade in the woods and sang out: "Look sharp, boys, don't fire too soon nor too high. Wait until they get to the creek."

The Confederates approached slowly and in magnificent order, and after the first volley of our men they sent a strong volley in return. Our men, now standing, fired twice more, then the Confederates charged through the creek, screaming savagely, and someone shouted:

"Run for your lives, boys!"

In fact, our small regiments were attacked by a force, apparently a hundred times larger, not alone in front, but also from the right side of our position. They came on running to surround us.

Our men fell back through the light woods just when brave General Ames, on foot, but in front of his Brigade, marched into the woods. He found them full of screaming Southerners, and after a volley his men, of course, had to run out also. Orders were shouted to fall back through Gettysburg on to Cemetery Hill, and it was high time to do so, as from all sides Confederate masses approached the town on the double quick.

Brave General Barlow about this time received a shot and fell from his horse. I rode behind our men into the town and saw many captured by Greycoats everywhere.

It was presumed that Barlow had been mortally wounded and he was left for dead on the field. He was found and cared for by Confederate Brig. Gen. John B. Gordon.—Ed. 2016

Passing a church on the outskirts, Surgeon Schultz, frightened to death, stopped me and asked if he would be taken prisoner, if caught. I said:

"Put a white handkerchief on your arm, and attend to the wounded. There are lots of them in the streets."

This delayed me and some twenty Confederates came rushing on, halloing to me to surrender. One excited fellow got hold of Caesar's bridle with his left hand and was ready to plunge his bayonet into me with the right, screaming: "Surrender! get down, you damned Yank!"

"You be damned," I answered, and cut off his hand with my Saxon sword. Then I started off, gave spurs to my horse, but to my horror found myself in a yard, surrounded by high fence rails. They shot at me from behind and demanded surrender.

"Marie!" I gasped, "save me!" And Caesar, with an enormous effort, jumped the fence and made off towards Cemetery Hill. Reaching the Arch, I dismounted and examined my horse; the poor fellow had been shot twice, but they were only slight flesh wounds. My left leg was wounded, and I felt the blood filling my right boot. My left shoulder strap had been shot away and the shoulder was badly scratched. One bullet had damaged the back of my saddle, partially protected by a rubber blanket, and when I tried to replace my sabre, I found the scabbard bent. I had hurt my right knee badly on the fence, and torn off one of my stirrups.

I sat down, pulled off the left boot and found a slight but painful flesh wound above the ankle. After binding my handkerchief around it, I drew the boot on again, suffering great pain, and mounted with much difficulty.

Meeting some staff officers, I asked: "Who attacked our Division?"

"General Ewell's whole Corps!"

No wonder that our small Brigade, with but one other in reserve, could not stop him. I now inquired where our men should take position. "Bight here behind the walls," I was told.

Soon I saw men with our Division sign on their caps running about, and I placed them behind the low stone walls. I had seen General Schimmelpfennig rushing into a house in Gettysburg, and I heard afterwards that he had remained three days concealed in a water tank in the yard. I saw my friend, Captain von Haake, taken prisoner, and Colonel von Gilsa I had noticed riding furiously out of town.

Soon General Ames stopped near me, cool and manly in appearance, though exhausted.

"We did our best, General," I said, "but Ewell must have had fifty times more men than we, and I think that we were posted entirely too far out. When they began to surround us, we had too long a run from our position to this place of retreat, and I am afraid that we have lost three-quarters of our men, killed, wounded, or captured. In town I heard nothing but 'Surrender!' and I was nearly caught myself, but this good horse saved me."

"See how your poor horse bleeds," he said.

"I know, but they are only flesh wounds, and I have some of the same sort myself."

"You did well with the skirmish line, and I heard you encourage the men. What is that blood on your sword?"

"Oh, I cut a Confederate's hand off, when he seized my bridle and halloed: 'Surrender, you damned Yank!' He probably damns me now still more!"

As the General looked at my sword, I added: "This fine sword blade is made of Damascus steel; it is as sharp as a razor, it bends but never breaks." So saying, I bent it into a circle and it jumped back perfectly straight.

"I inherited it from a granduncle," I continued, "who served as a Cavalry General under Napoleon First, and who performed heroic deeds with its aid. I had the blade reset when I became a Cavalry officer in Europe, and they expressed it to me a few months ago from Germany."

Another squad of men now reached us. They were breathless, and I told them to lie behind the wall and rest. By seven o'clock we had several hundred men of the Division together.

"General Barlow lies wounded outside of Gettysburg," the General said, "and I take command of the Division. You'd better stay with me, Captain." Ames

"Thanks, General," I returned. "Here comes Mrs. [Arabella] Barlow with an ambulance," I added, and we both approached her, and tried to describe where her husband could probably be found. The courageous lady, sitting next to the driver, with a white flag in her hand, then drove quickly towards the town, although we could still hear firing. Colonel von Gilsa did not reach us until about ten that night, as he had lost his way and reached Robinson's First Corps Brigade before he found us.

"You can now command your Brigade easily with the voice, my dear Colonel," I said, "this is all that is left," pointing to a few flags, each surrounded by a handful of sleeping and dusty men. "General Ames is in command of the Division and wants me."

"Well, come to see a fellow sometimes," he said, as he dismounted and lay down very much fatigued. I, though not less tired, had to go from regiment to regiment and get reports, and, at last, fearfully exhausted, lay down on the ground about midnight, holding poor Caesar by the halter strap.

Frankel, contrary to his usual custom, was not to be seen, when I awoke at three o'clock, and being afraid that Caesar might give out, I asked permission to ride to the ambulances, where the man had orders to remain. He was sleeping soundly when I arrived, but a light kick made him jump up.

"Get me some coffee, quick, and some cigars," I said.

64

He looked about, and seeing a cook near a fire, coaxed him to let me have a tin cup of coffee, which tasted like nectar.

An assistant surgeon nearby, who knew me, woke up, and I begged him to look at my leg. He washed the wound, and put plasters over it, while Frankel was rubbing my right knee with spirits of camphor. Caesar's wounds had stopped bleeding and were washed, while he ate some hay.

For money and some good words, I then succeeded in having my canteen filled with black coffee, and took a hand full of crackers out of a box.

"You stay here to-day, Frankel," I said, "or go to a safe place, as I can't afford to have all my horses damaged—feed up the U. S. horse well." Stiff, worn out Caesar, carried me at a lazy gallop back to Cemetery Hill, where I refreshed the General with some coffee and crackers, handing the rest to the grateful von Gilsa.

CHAPTER VI.

The sun had risen, and from the high position where we stood, about a hundred feet from the Arch, and on the highest point of Cemetery Hill, we had a magnificent view. Before us lay Gettysburg; behind the walls, down the hill and fronting our right, were our men. Wherever you looked, regiments upon regiments were marching into position. Large open fields were on the right; on Benner's Hill and across Rock Creek, Confederate batteries stood next to each other in imposing numbers. The position of the Eleventh Corps was near the Baltimore Pike, and our Division was on the extreme right. Next to us and at our rear were located all the batteries of the First and Eleventh Corps. I rode about and looked at the position on the Ridge.

Schurz's Division was posted in front of Evergreen Cemetery, on the left of the Baltimore Pike, and I considered it safe, as Captain Dilger's Battery was stationed nearby, in Ziegler's Grove, I believe. On our right I found a Division of the First Corps, in touch with the Twelfth. With the spy-glass I saw Confederate troops forming in Gettysburg, and outposts were visible in front, and on our right. We were certainly well posted, and our Artillery had a fine chance to fire in all directions. Everything remained quiet, except that slight changes were made in the positions; plenty of cartridges were distributed, and, now and then, a box of crackers was carried to a starved regiment. Only from time to time a shot was fired from the steeple of that very church, where Surgeon Schultz got me into a scrape, and two officers were wounded. One of the sharpshooters seemed to be especially after me, for whenever I rose a bullet whistled close by me.

"Why not drive these rascals out, General?" I asked.

"General Howard has some sharpshooters," he answered. "Ask him to let them return the fire."

I found General Howard in the Cemetery, and soon twelve men with the finest rifles, lay behind the wall near us, and bang went their bullets through the small openings of the church tower. After some twenty shots, we saw the fellows run out of the church, and one dropped down from a last, well-directed shot of our *tirailleurs*, while another was carried away wounded.

Our sharpshooters were Swiss boys, well-armed with the finest telescope rifles. Of course we watched the right closely, and about four o'clock I announced that the Confederates were preparing to fire. Twelve batteries opened on us, every shot being directed at Cemetery Hill. Our batteries replied with great rapidity and accuracy, as I could see through my spy-glass. Caissons exploded, and horses were thrown down in numbers.

For two hours we had to stand quiet, listening to the noise, and seeing men and horses killed around us, but it was a grand sight nevertheless, the air around us literally full of whizzing balls.

At five o'clock, a man lying behind the wall called out to me: "Look at your horse, sir!"

I turned around and found that a piece of a shell had torn away poor Caesar's nose! The poor fellow stood there trembling, his long lower jaw exposed. It gave me a shock, as the sight was horrible. Stepping near him, I pushed his head down and fired a bullet from my revolver behind his ear; he dropped, but was not dead, so I had to shoot twice more before he gave a last convulsive shudder. I shall never forget the look he gave me before I fired the first time; it seemed to say: "What made you bring me back; here, after I saved your life?"'"

The tremendous shelling continued until half past six, then it seemed that the Confederate batteries were silenced, but we saw large columns approaching us. In splendid order they came marching through the cornfield, and impetuously they charged Colonel von Gilsa's Brigade, screaming: "We are the Louisiana Tigers!" Our men fired in good time, and their bullets told, but on came the enemy—more and more of them, climbing the wall and forcing the Brigade up the hill behind the batteries.

Now our batteries began to fire grape and canister, but some brave fellows came up to one of the batteries and demanded surrender; the battery men, assisted by General Ames, two officers and myself, cut them down. With hand-spikes and rammers the cannoniers struck at their heads, and my good sword behaved well again. All who had' reached the battery were killed, then the guns were reloaded and rapidly fired, and we stood sur-rounded by dense smoke.

General Schurz had sent a Brigade to reinforce us, and hearing them advance, I joined and charged with them down the hill. They drove the Confederates back over the wall and then we lay down as our cannons were firing very close over our heads. When they at last stopped firing we saw the enemy flying over the fields, and noticed a Brigade of the First Corps, which had nobly assisted us in the charge. Lest another attack should follow, our position was now somewhat strengthened, and our men were again placed behind the wall.

It had been a furious attack, and lasted nearly an hour. The wounded were cared for, and the dead thrown in a ditch.

We heard later that over sixteen hundred Louisiana Tigers and other men were slain. Our loss was remarkably small, and, as usual, our Batteries had done the butchering.

I was unhurt, except for a blow between the stomach and chest given me by one of our men with the butt of a gun, when I had tried to stop him, after the first onslaught. The blow was so severe that I fell down quite faint from it, and they were ready to carry me away, but I soon recollected the incident, and much enraged, told the story, and only asked for a drink of water to ease the pain. In vain did I look for that scoundrel, after everything was quiet, and considering how enraged I was, it was lucky for him that I did not recognize him.

The excitement and my exertions had been great, and I was prostrated from fatigue and hunger, when at ten o'clock Frankel arrived and brought me some fried liver and crackers. All the others were sleeping soundly around me, and I began to eat slowly, but fell asleep, and waking up at daybreak, found myself still holding some greasy pieces in my hand.

On July 3d at five o'clock, we heard heavy Infantry firing on our right, but only part of our skirmishers had a chance to come near enough to the attacking party to fire.

At one o'clock a terrific cannonade opened upon us, offering a still grander spectacle than yesterday's bombardment. I counted fourteen Batteries sending shells and balls on the Ridge, and I understand that at one time sixteen Batteries were firing.

Our Batteries were answering, the air was filled with deadly missiles, and, as not an inch of ground offered the slightest safety, I told the nervous men to stay just where they were, as they could be struck in one place as well as another, if it was so written.

I witnessed some terrible scenes, saw six horses killed by the explosion of one shell, and, at one time, a whole group of men killed and wounded together. During the heaviest fire I was lucky enough to make the terrified men cheer once. I had been sent over to Schurz, who was stationed across the Baltimore Pike, west of us. I stopped there a short while, after delivering my order, and saw some fine shots fired by my ideal of a hero, Captain Hubert Dilger, who, more than any General, deserved the gratitude of our Corps, and was more than any other man connected with the army, entitled to rapid promotion.

"He should be honored with a monument," I thought. "He is as brave as was once Pulaski, as competent and gallant as Baron de Kalb, who fell at Camden, South Carolina, during the Revolutionary War, and as true a gentleman as ever lived." Looking about, I said aloud:

"After this bombardment you will be attacked again. See, Dilger, how they are already forming behind that fence, about twelve hundred yards away."

He looked, aimed his guns, and ordered: "Fire!" And that very fence was shot to pieces in no time. Many must have been killed and wounded, and their companions' courage to charge, later on, must have been greatly subdued. I then hurried away to join my command.

69

After recrossing the road to Gettysburg, and while mounting Cemetery Hill, many voices screamed at me:

"Look out! Look out!"

I did not understand why, but by intuition I made a big jump to the left, and then was loudly cheered.

It turned out that a twenty-pound shell came ricocheting directly towards me, and would have torn my legs away had I not jumped. They all admired my presence of mind, but I murmured to myself: "Thanks to thee, my Guardian Angel, my Marie!"

Before three, this grand bombardment ceased, and again on came the infantry regiments, charging mostly the positions west of us, but this time before we could order our regiments to fire, the batteries, with their grape and canister, broke the enemy's lines and made them run. This was their last attack, and during the night they withdrew.

On the 4th of July we remained in our position and took things easier, as the main danger seemed to be over. I visited some wounded officers at the hospital tents, and witnessed many amputations while there, in order to become acquainted with all the horrors of war. Piles of legs and arms lay near the operating stone, and still the surgeons cut away.

In the afternoon I rode into Gettysburg, was shaved and had my photograph taken, wearing Miss Kate Chase's rich and large shoulder-straps and a braided jacket; gold stripes on the pants, two golden half-moons, the sign of the Eleventh Corps, on the collar, and extra richly gilded buttons.

The stench on Cemetery Hill was terrible. The rain and sun had decomposed men and horses quickly, and the General and myself kept as far away as possible.

About five o'clock some citizen told me that quite a number of Confederates were in a barn a quarter of a mile out of town. I rode there, knocked with my sword at the door, and called out that they would better surrender, as General Lee had gone long ago. A Captain peeped out and said:

"We are ready to surrender, sir," and I ordered him and twenty-three men to fall in line and marched them through Gettysburg to headquarters, where I turned them over to the Provost Marshal. The poor fellows were starved, and glad to become prisoners, and although I may have been somewhat rash in going out all alone and asking them to give themselves into my hands, still, as it happened, there was no real danger.

On the evening of the fifth we marched to Rock Creek, where we camped. On July 7th to High Knobb; on July 8th to Middletown; then we took a position near Boonesboro; then near Beaver Creek; and on July 12th at four o'clock in the morning our Division was ordered to Hagerstown to support Kilpatrick's Cavalry.

General Judson Kilpatrick, known as "Kill Cavalry."—Ed. 2016

We had some skirmishing there, and took over a hundred prisoners, driving the force out of town. This capture of Hagerstown was mere fun, still we lost one man killed and four wounded, after General Kilpatrick had, in full view of us, charged a Confederate cavalry camp. Having placed pickets, the staff went to the Female Seminary, where Colonel von Gilsa played waltzes on the piano, and we young fellows danced with the girls, to the very amusing disgust and horror of the old lady principal.

About five o'clock a shell struck and exploded on the top of the house. The girls were hurried into the cellar, while we rushed to the Command; but it seemed to have been only a farewell greeting, as, after sending out a reconnoitering party, we found that the enemy had crossed on a bridge at Falling Waters and forded the Potomac, where many were drowned.

So we were safe. The whole of the Eleventh Corps came through Hagerstown on the fifteenth. We joined them and marched to Berlin, where, on the sixteenth, we took a position.

I had caught a severe cold during the last few days, and was suffering from bronchitis. Besides this, my knee, which had been hurt at Gettysburg, became badly inflamed through much riding, and the light flesh wounds were very sore and painful. General Howard's Adjutant-General had heard about my condition and

71

ordered me to bring the 153d Pennsylvania, whose time was out, to Easton, Pennsylvania, and to remain on leave of absence until well again and fit for duty.

From Easton, after seeing the regiment mustered out, I went to Bethlehem, and, meeting there the wives of Generals Siegel and Schurz, Colonel Gilsa and those of other officers of the Eleventh Corps, I was most kindly greeted, but I grew worse and was very ill. After a severe fever I became so weak that my pulse almost ceased beating, and the troubles created by my fall on the saddle knob at Chancellorsville created much pain. The doctor said that overexertion and neglect of bodily injuries was the cause.

Everybody expected that I would die. Mrs. Governor Reeder, of Easton, heard of my condition, and as I was a friend of her two sons, Howard and Frank, both gallant officers in the Army, she drove over to Bethlehem and insisted that I should come to her home, where I could find more comforts and better medical attendance. The care taken of me there was actually touching, and that noble lady, her daughter, and some of their friends managed, assisted by the family physician, to restore me. Then we drove to Schooley's Mountain, where Mrs. Reeder's other daughter, Mrs. Marsh, resided, and the mountain air did me so much good that three weeks later I felt strong enough to report at my Command. Altogether I had been on leave two months.

In Washington I was told that the 68th New York now belonged to Colonel Kryzanowsky's Brigade and Schurz's Division, and that General Schurz's present headquarters were at Warrenton Junction.

I returned well equipped, and brought a barrel of lager beer on the sutler's wagon I had hired at the station. This insured my welcome at these headquarters, and as I brought the General a letter from his beautiful wife and news of his children, he con- descended to treat me decently, and allowed me to remain a few days in his Adjutant's tent, until I could find out where Frankel and my horses were, and on whose staff I was next to do duty.

In the evening we had a regular feast, and some wild turkeys shot by Captain Tiedeman were served in good style. We drank to the good *Pontet Canet* I had brought, and later on tapped the barrel of lager beer. Of course, we talked war after I had related my experiences East. General Schurz said casually that he had heard my conduct at Chancellorsville and Gettysburg well-spoken of, and Captain Dilger added:

"Yes, it is a pity that Baron von Fritsch did not arrive in this country sooner, and that he did not organize a Cavalry Regiment. From him we should have had more reliable news."

Company A, 68th New York, consisted, when I inspected it, of twenty-nine men, and surely needed no Captain, and I was not anxious for such a small command. The next day in camp brought me some disagreeable surprises. General Schimmelpfennig's Quartermaster, a man named Hagen, had shown me some kindness during the last campaign, as von Gilsa's Quartermaster was a brute, and very stingy with oats and hay; so when I left the command at Berlin I told Frankel that he would better remain with Hagen, and the latter promised to see to it that my horses should look well when I returned.

But General Schimmelpfennig had been ordered with his Brigade to South Carolina, and there, under palms and in sugar cane fields, were probably my horses. This was a bad fix, and I may as well state right here that Hagen was forced out of service while at Charleston, and that up to the present time I have never heard a word about Frankel, nor my horses, saddles, etc. I wrote, but received no answer of any sort, and as we soon left camp again I counted the loss among the casualties of war.

Hagen had no right to take my horses along when his Brigade became detached from the Corps, and should have left my property with the Brigade to which my Regiment belonged. As my valuable Caesar was dead, I lost only two horses, and my three saddles, bridles, etc.

My capital had been again severely taxed, and I had only two thousand dollars in bank. I returned to camp with some five hundred dollars in my pocket. I had brought with me, from the East, a new saddle and outfit, and I began to look around for a charger. A

Lieutenant-Colonel who was going-home to "mamma," as the Governor had appointed an outsider over him as Colonel, sold me a very fine, large sorrel, which we christened, with great ceremony, Caesar, although there was no similarity in color.

I also captured a fine looking, bright, colored boy to wait on me. This negro was like all the others in the South—lazy, dreaming, and only waking up to say: "Boss, please let me have a quarter." But I made up my mind to improve him, and spared no money in dressing him well. I forced him to clean himself twice a day, under my supervision, which consisted in using the riding whip pretty often. I licked him into one of the best servants a man could have. I called him Tom, and he stuck to me well, cleaned my big boots without falling asleep, was good to Caesar, and learned to do things on a trot.

Tom inspired, later on, many Southern citizen with rage by his appearance. He had learned to walk straight, to wear polished boots, was dressed in an improved army fatigue suit, had a small hat on with a red, white and blue ribbon around it, always sported a clean handkerchief, sticking outside his coat pocket, and looked well washed and groomed. He would speak to no one but me, and became my shadow. Where I was, one could always see Tom, at a respectful distance. I was often complimented by other officers for breaking in and training this former savage so well. I was interested in him enough to teach him German, and to let him learn how to write, and the fellow improved wonderfully fast. At the end of six weeks I addressed him in German entirely, and he wrote some words with ease.

Not having interacted with African-Americans before, many northerners and immigrants wrote of being astonished at their voracious appetites for education once they were allowed to learn. Teaching slaves to read and write was illegal in most of the south.—Ed. 2016

He could read a little when I got him, but in a short time made great progress, as I devoted at least two hours a day to his education. After six weeks of training he seldom needed a thrashing, and, as time passed, not at all. He had become a faithful, attentive, lively and careful valet and groom.

"I'll never leave you, Captain, while I am alive," he often said, "and if I don't do right, just lick me hard. I'm done with these lazy people South, and want to be 'way up' servant." A few days later, at General Schurz's headquarters, I was delighted to hear that orders had come from Washington for the Eleventh and Twelfth Corps to proceed at once to Nashville, Tennessee, under command of General Joseph Hooker, in order to assist General Rosecrans, who found himself in a state of siege. A large Confederate army was at his front, and the precipitate hills on which Nashville is built, at the rear.

The battle of Chickamauga had just been fought, and it had been the hardest and bloodiest in the South, and although General Bragg claimed a great victory, Chattanooga, the great gateway of the mountains, remained in the possession of the Army of the Cumberland, which Rosecrans commanded, and General Bragg had paid a heavy price for his victory.

But now the whole Union Army had retired within the works of Chattanooga, and General Longstreet's Corps occupied Lookout Valley, cutting off all communication with Bridgeport, and it became impossible to send supplies to the army. General Rosecrans and his four thousand men were starving, and now General Hooker, with some fifteen thousand men, was ordered to hurry to his relief as fast as rails could take him.

On September 24th we commenced the long voyage of eighteen hundred miles, and I was placed in charge of the transportation of Colonel Kryzanowsky's Brigade. He had now the 68th New York in his command, and cheerfully took me on his staff. The first order handed to me was one issued by General Halleck in Washington, and the Commander-in-Chief wished us to understand that any officer interfering with the railroad officials or their arrangements would be immediately dismissed from the service. So my new position was not an enviable one.

Forty to sixty men were packed into each cattle car, still smelling of manure, and very poor accommodations were offered to the General and the other officers. As I could not kick, I tried "soft soap," and sometimes improved the first arrangements by getting a few cars more, and a passenger car for officers.

How we got the two Corps alive to Nashville in seven days it is difficult to explain, as our men were so crowded, had so little chance to obtain water or food, and, locked lip in the cars, had neither fresh air enough nor even the ordinary necessities of life. But we got there, and our Brigade was immediately reshipped to Bridgeport, Alabama, where we camped for a few days, and were able to take a good bath in the Tennessee River.

They stationed us at first to guard the Chattanooga Railroad against attacks of the Confederate Cavalry, who were nearby in the mountains, while supplies were; being accumulated at Stevenson, Alabama, awaiting the opening of communication with the army at Chattanooga.

We all knew "Old Rosy," as the boys called General Rosecrans, by reputation. He was beloved by his men, a good General, but very independent. We were anxious to assist him and regretted the delay.

"*Himmel! Kreuz! Donnerwetter!*" I would exclaim, when the new orders were only for a little scout into the hills and forests. "Why won't they let us drive Longstreet away?"

News now reached us that General Rosecrans had been relieved, and I had the honor of shaking his hand at Bridgeport. All he would say was:

"You will have to fight under Grant now, boys, I am going home to Cincinnati to rest."

From a general order I learned that Major-General Ulysses S. Grant had been placed in command of the Military Division of the Mississippi, and concluded that the troops on the Tennessee were under him. Rumors also reached us that General Grant had ordered his friend, General Sherman, to join him, and that the Eleventh and Twelfth Corps had been consolidated, but this was not correct, and the Eleventh had only assumed the name of "Howard's Corps." He being, since his selection of Cemetery Hill at Gettysburg, a great General and in good standing at Washington.

Grant's great victory at Vicksburg, which gave the Union control of the Mississippi, came on July 4, 1863, just one day after Meade's victory at Gettysburg.—Ed. 2016

"Those Dutchmen" under Carl Schurz had run like cowards at Chancellorsville, in spite of General Howard's tactics and precautions, and poor General Devens had been forced to retreat in great disorder when an overwhelming force attacked him, because he found no support in Carl Schurz's Division.

Questioning seriously who the devil I was now, I concluded that I was a Captain of the 68th New York, detached as an aid-de-camp to the gallant Colonel Wladimir Kryzanowsky, who commanded a Brigade in Schurz's Division of Howard's Corps.

General Howard was placed under General Hooker. I meditated, "Hooker under General Thomas, Thomas under General Grant, Grant, under General Halleck, Halleck under Secretary Stanton, Stanton under the great War President, His Excellency President Lincoln, Commander-in-Chief of all the United States, armies, the noblest of them all."

On March 3, 1864 Lincoln promoted Grant to Lieutenant General, giving him command of all Union Armies, under direct supervision only to the President.—Ed. 2016

At last marching orders came, and on October 28, 1863, we had advanced to Lookout Valley, our Division first. Soon we ran against pickets of the Southern army and drove them away, after killing a few outposts. We marched on and in the afternoon were surprised by sharp volleys of musketry from a wooded ridge. We wheeled around and before our General could prevent it, charged and drove the enemy from their cover, but let them run away unmolested. We then resumed our march, after burying four dead and sending eight wounded to the rear.

Near Brown's Ferry we were allowed to camp. About midnight we were aroused from sleep and ordered to march at once. Longstreet had just attacked Hooker's command and we had to fight desperately in the dark till after four in the morning, when the Southerners fell back to their fortified camp in Chattanooga Valley.

This remarkable battle near Wauhatchie, Tennessee, on October 28, 1863, proved the material the Eleventh Corps was made of, and should always be remembered with pride by the whole nation. The greatest bravery was shown on both sides and the charge of Colonel Smith's brigade of Steinwehr's division of the Eleventh Corps up an almost inaccessible mountain in face of a firing enemy (known as the battle in the clouds), was, without doubt, the most heroic during the entire war. With their bayonets only they drove Longstreet's brave veterans out of their intrenchments on the top of a hill, which tourists now can hardly climb, assisted by alpine sticks.

Never before and never afterwards has such extraordinary gallantry been shown by any of the American troops. General Grant, General Hooker and others watched those brave fellows climbing up and expressed in loud terms their greatest admiration.

Howard's Corps then joined the Army of the Cumberland under General Thomas. A demonstration in force, in order to make the wagon road from Bridgeport, Alabama, through Lookout Valley and the narrow gorge to Brown's Ferry, the channel of reinforcements as well as of supplies, was ordered at once. We advanced rapidly, driving several pickets away until we came to a mound called Orchard Knob, which was occupied by a large Confederate force. Our brave boys charged the little hill before an order could be given, and, after some strong resistance and some hand to hand fighting, drove the enemy away. My remarkably brave and strong charger brought me almost first to the top of the hill, and a young, good-looking Southern cavalier on horseback fired at me with his revolver. Again my protecting angel, "Marie," saved me, and the ball passed close to my left ear. Sword in hand, I spurred my horse towards him, and before he could fire a second time, I cut him in the right arm, which caused him to drop his weapon. I demanded his surrender, and he replied:

"I am afraid that I will have to give up," dismounting at the same time.

"Lead that officer to some surgeon and ask him for immediate attendance to his wound," I said to a couple of men. To my astonishment the prisoner exclaimed:

"Thanks, Baron!" and another look convinced me that it was a young gentleman, whose name I could not recollect just then, but I remembered having met him at the St. Charles Hotel in New Orleans in 1860. Of course, I had no time to talk to him, as my assistance was needed to secure the surrender of many other Confederates. After this little episode, I expected that we would be ordered to attack Missionary Ridge, about four hundred feet high, but an order came from General Grant that we should hurry to the assistance of General Sherman, commanding the Army of the Tennessee, and off we tramped.

From a hill I could later watch the magnificent assault of the Army of the Cumberland on Missionary Ridge. The regiments, much larger than ours, advanced, marching as on parade, while forty to fifty cannons were sending their deathly missiles at and over them. They climbed the Ridge with wonderful energy and heroism.

I was told afterwards, that this brilliant charge occasioned some fun at Headquarters.

When General Grant noticed it, he trotted over to General Thomas and said, in a rather excited way: "General, who ordered those troops to charge Missionary Ridge?"

General Thomas, after throwing a careful and kind look on his beloved regiments, replied:

"I am sorry to say, General, that I did not," and then, turning to some other Major-Generals near him inquired of each if he did. All denied having given such an order, and then Thomas said quietly "General Grant, it seems to me that they started of their own free will."

General Grant watched them for some time, then rushing up the hill, lit a fresh cigar, and said: "If this turns out well, all right; if not, someone will have to suffer for it."

It turned out well, the boys got to the top, drove the enemy away, captured cannons, ammunition, prisoners, and camp material, and then gave three cheers for "Pap" Thomas.

After we had reached the Army of the Tennessee, they were attacked by the right wing of the Confederates, and at first both sides held out well. Then we marched forward, and, after a most sturdy resistance, drove the enemy away in great disorder.

Scarcely rested, we were ordered to Knoxville, East Tennessee, to relieve Burnside; but when we reached there Longstreet's forces, who had probably heard that they would have to fight the glorious remnant of one of the bravest and finest Corps of the Army of the Potomac, thought best to retire in a hurry, and thus we ended the long siege of Knoxville, thank God, without shedding a drop of blood.

Then we returned to Lookout Valley, and reached a very poor old camp, in a most deplorable condition. We were in rags, boots and shoes torn or burned to pieces, everybody more or less sick, terribly worn out and starved. We found very little to eat, as the Commissary had not expected us so soon. Old hardtacks, covered with mould, a little bacon, and, fortunately, some coffee were distributed in ridiculously small rations.

The weather was beastly. It rained all the time, and a cold wind blew down the valley day and night. I had contracted a very severe case of bronchial catarrh, and lying on a wet blanket in a dog tent, without a rag to close up the front entrance, my condition became a very serious one. I was coughing continually, spitting out a greenish-gray substance, and suffering great pain. My head, resting on a log, became considerably swollen by the continual effort to clear my throat, and my eyes began to hurt me badly. As all the doctors were sick themselves, and my servant had not shown up, I had to care for myself. I placed the bacon issued me around my neck, and covered my chest with it; the mouldy hardtack I used as a pillow and kept alive for several days by inhaling the fumes of the hot coffee brought to me by a cook twice a day.

Some officers in shelter tents near mine finally notified General Schurz of my condition, and he kindly called and said: "You would better try to get to some hospital, Captain, or you will surely die. I will send you an order for the Nashville hospital."

I had become so weak that in trying to get to the nearest railway station I sometimes had to crawl on all fours. But I managed to climb into an empty freight car, and reached the yards at Nashville the next morning about six o'clock. With great trouble I worked my way between immensely long rows of cars and reached the hospital at nine in the morning. They cleaned me up with warm water and soap, gave me a night shirt, and put me to bed. The warm, dry air in the room soothed my sufferings wonderfully, and by next morning I coughed less. Soon I improved by the kind care given to me by a beautiful Northern maiden.

Sixteen days later, pale as a ghost, and still weak, I returned to my command, now clean and' warmly dressed, with my sword well-polished, my-revolvers free of rust, and I was ordered to super--intend the building of some corduroy roads.

CHAPTER VII.

The three years' term of service of the brave, glorious, reduced and much tramped about 68th Regiment of New York Volunteers had now expired, and we were allowed to go home.

Colonel Bourry had been cashiered, as was to be expected, and Lieutenant-Colonel von Steinhausen, for a long time a Southern prisoner, had command of the Regiment. We were shipped to Louisville first, paid off and mustered out, then we proceeded to New York City, together with the 58th New York.

There we were received with great honors. New York knew that we had served faithfully for three years, and that our flags, showing hundreds of bullet holes, and consisting of little torn strips, deserved recognition. Several militia regiments turned out and escorted us up Broadway, after we had passed in review before the Mayor. We looked sunburnt, rough, badly clad, and we were few in numbers. Out of twelve hundred and ninety men only hundred and thirty-eight of the 68th returned. The cheering of the crowd, the bouquets and garlands thrown by the ladies, made me feel sad, I don't know exactly why. Still, straight as an arrow, I marched in front of my little Company A, somewhat lame, looking battle worn, but strong and hardy. I was literally covered with flowers and gay ribbons before we reached Grand street, and there they marched us—probably because we were Germans—to a Bowery saloon, where we could eat and drink, free, the whole day and night.

I took French leave at once, and went to the Fifth Avenue Hotel, where my trunks, checked in 1862 at Willard's Hotel, had arrived. They had been claimed soon after by a friend, who now forwarded them. The next day I looked presentable, and commenced with care and in earnest, to learn how to eat once more a square meal, something better than crackers or fresh pork, and to drink coffee out of a china, instead of a tin cup.

Oh, how I enjoyed that first breakfast! How carefully I ordered the first dinner! How delightful it was to sleep in a bed again! After a few days I was feeling better, but somehow I was always sad. I spoke to no one. Marie was constantly in my mind, with her halo of blonde hair, her soft, expressive eyes, and her tender mouth. I thanked her for having so wonderfully protected me on the battlefield, and for having led me safely through all perils; I thanked her for the present bliss and comforts of civilization. Sometimes moved to tears, I spent hours in my room, after a long rest during the night, smoking and thinking of her.

And so one week passed. Then I concluded to move to cheaper quarters, and I came in contact again with officers and men of the 68th who wanted to re-enlist. In spite of my sad experiences, I re-enlisted with the others. Once more I became Captain of Company A, of the 68th Regiment, now Veteran Volunteers.

While in New York I did everything to strengthen my constitution by careful, though rich living. I called once on Mr. August Belmont,* to whom I had been strongly recommended by the Rothschilds in Frankfort, to ask him to favor me with a few lines to Governor Seymour, his strong Democratic friend. He kindly gave me a good letter, and if I had been clever I would have left at once and alone for Albany, and would no doubt have secured for myself a commission as Major in my Regiment, or in some Cavalry Regiment; but, being too good natured and too unselfish for that, I used the letter for Captain Arnold Kummer's promotion.

August Belmont, Sr. (1813 – 1890) was German-American politician, financier, foreign diplomat, and party chairman of the Democratic National Committee during the 1850s. He was later a horse-breeder and racehorse owner who built the Belmont Park racecourse on Long Island, New York.—Ed. 2016

He and Lieutenant-Colonel von Steinhausen went with me to Albany to protest against the appointment of Felix, Prince Salm-Salm, late Colonel of the 8th New York, who had, before we reached New York, secured for himself the Colonelcy of our regiment, in case we should re-enlist. His beautiful wife had done the talking—and a good deal of smiling and coaxing—as he had never learned to speak the English language fluently.

Interestingly, when they met and fell in love, she could not speak German and he could not speak English.—Ed. 2016

The Governor received us, and I let Steinhausen speak to him, but he had no success at all, and the Governor stated that he had come too late, as Salm had received the commission some time ago. Then I advanced and presented Mr. Belmont's letter. The Governor changed his tone at once, cordially grasped my hand, and said:

"Very glad to meet you. What can I do for you, sir?"

"Nothing at present, Governor, but I beg of you to make Captain Kummer, Major of the Regiment. He is engaged to a lady in Baltimore, who nurse I him in the hospital, and only wants the title of Major. He will soon resign, and then I beg you to favor me with that rank."

He ordered this promotion at once. Captain Kummer had asked me to do this, and had promised me that he would resign inside of four weeks. After reaching camp he cut my acquaintance, and served on.

Prince Salm-Salm was Colonel Steinhausen, Lieutenant-Colonel; Kummer, Major, and I, Senior Captain.

The newly reorganized regiment was partially filled up with drafted men and substitutes. Salm kept away from us, and his wife worked in Washington to have him, later on, promoted to a Brigadier-Generalship.

We returned to Lookout Valley without a Colonel. Encamped on a hill, we served as Guard for the Quartermaster and Commissary Departments, and our men stood sentinels near hay bales, and cracker boxes, shoes and dry goods. As our regimental Quartermaster was acting Brigade Quartermaster, I made myself Regimental Quartermaster, in order to be entitled to a horse, and as such was kept fairly busy.

We heard nothing of the army doings, and did not know to what Command we belonged. I found out, somehow, that General Howard had been given the command of the Fourth Army Corps, and that Hooker had formed a corps out of the old Eleventh and Twelfth, now called the Twentieth.

84

By and by they thought of us, and we were placed in a Division commanded by General Steedman for the defence of the Nashville and Chattanooga Railroad.

We were brought by rail to Bridgeport, Alabama, and, as Steinhausen gave me the choice, I selected the most important position, that of Commander of the Detachment, east of the Tennessee River, and I took the responsibility on myself of keeping the railroad and pontoon bridges over the Tennessee safe against raids of the enemy.

Regimental headquarters were established on an island formed by the Tennessee River, and two more Captains commanded other Detachments. Engineers had built a magnificent, very large and strong blockhouse for me, between the two bridges, which I occupied with one hundred and twenty men of the 68th Regiment, and I had six guns furnished. I placed pickets and outposts, drilled the Detachment in firing through the loop holes, and in handling the twelve-pounders.

As the blockhouse was very damp and badly ventilated, I allowed the men to live in tents during the day, and built for myself a nice little wooden cottage, inside of some earth-works, close to the river, under some magnificent trees.

A large barn, used by the engineers, I transformed into a stable, and bought two nice cows, a couple of pigs, and two chicken coops from a farmer who wanted to move away. My men picked up, besides, a lame, but very pretty, little mule, in the woods nearby, turned loose probably by some quartermaster as unfit to pull with one of the many teams which had gone up to Chattanooga.

The little brute had the left hind ankle badly damaged from being entangled in a chain, it seemed, and I went to work to cure him as well as possible. Salves and bandages were applied continually by Tom, who was soon on intimate terms with the mule. Besides, I had the fine sorrel horse, and after getting a good cooking stove, some furniture and bedding from Nashville, I was fixed better than any General in the field at least, and owned quite a farm.

I frequently scouted the neighborhood, and made the acquaintance of the nearest farmers, who all expressed the wish that the war would soon end, and showed most friendly feelings, one offering me, during my stay, a very nice buggy which he considered unsafe in his barn. Of course I did not trust them, and used two very brave and intelligent men of my command, dressed half as Confederates, and claiming to have belonged to Longstreet's Corps, as secret scouts in the mountains.

I lived very comfortably and well. A man named Sutter was an excellent cook, and prepared my meals, and at Bridgeport I could buy almost everything. Eggs, butter, vegetables, spring chickens and even game were brought daily to my headquarters by the farmer girls and boys from the mountains, who gladly exchanged them for coffee, sugar and salt. As they could not cross the bridges without my written permit, I always had the first pick.

Unfortunately we all, by and by, contracted a fever, living so near the swampy river, and sleeping at night in the blockhouse, and in one of my reports I had to state that every man in my Command shook once a day, and the Captain twice. This induced General Thomas to order the Commissary to furnish regular whiskey rations and lots of sauerkraut. Every man had to take quinine with his whiskey, and I lost only three men by death; the others soon grew better. Somehow or other I suffered from this fever for years.

Three or four times I captured suspicious persons on the hills, and once, at midnight, surrounded a camp of some twenty rebels, who all claimed to be discharged soldiers, but still had guns and wore uniforms. I believe that they were deserters, and I never saw more frightened fellows in all my life. They lay asleep in a nice grove, when I completely surrounded them and gave orders to fire away. We had a little moonlight, and could see them on their knees, with hands held high, imploring us:

"Don't fire, for God's sake. We surrender!" Triumphantly I marched them to our block- house, and sent them as prisoners to headquarters, capturing at the same time five horses, sixteen small arms and some belts and ammunition.

86

The bridges were never attacked, and the roads in my district remained in good condition. Train after train brought supplies to the troops in front, and large herds of cattle were driven over the pontoon bridges.

The most unpleasant day was when Prince Salm-Salm arrived on the island, followed by his wife, two other ladies, and some seven men, to whom he had promised commissions in the Regiment. The officers and men received him with sour faces, but as I had known him in Germany, when he was an officer in the Prussian Hussars, and he and I had moved during one Winter in the same society at Frankfort-on-the-Main, where he frequently led the cotillion, I was obliged to greet him in a friendly manner, and invited him, his ladies and suite, to dine at my cottage, placing my accommodations at his disposal until the Quartermaster was able to fix a place for him.

This gave me a chance at once to become acquainted with his most beautiful, charming and accomplished wife, of whose deeds of valor in former campaigns I had already heard, and who had many times attended the wounded on battlefields. She told me that they had come to Bridgeport, Alabama, directly from Washington, where she had succeeded in securing a private audience with our President, Mr. Abraham Lincoln. As I had once enjoyed the same great privilege, I asked her how he had acted.

"Oh, I had a splendid time with him. As soon as I entered his private office I asked his permission to embrace and kiss the greatest man our country had ever known since Washington, and he patted me kindly on the head, asking what he could do for me. 'I only came to see you, Mr. Lincoln, because I was most anxious to meet you. My husband, who was Colonel in the 8th New York, and is the bravest man in the army, was lately favored with a commission as Colonel of the 68th New York, as his Regiment's time was out. So we are all right, but he actually deserves to be made a General, he is such a dashing officer.'

"'And has such a pretty wife,' the President interposed.

"'How kind, Mr. President,' I said, and then coaxed him for a commission as Brigadier-General for Salm.

"'We have more Brigadiers now than soldiers,' he laughingly replied, 'but I will give you a few lines to General Thomas, who commands down there, and suggest to him to let the Prince have a Brigade, when he sees a chance, and at the same time authorize him to raise him to a Brevet-Brigadier, after he has specially distinguished himself.' "He then wrote a few lines and handed them to me. So we will not be long in your way of promotion, Baron, and you must be really good to us." She then shook hands with me and gave me one of the most charming, bewildering of smiles, with which she conquered all men, and I deeply regretted that she did not add an embrace and a kiss besides.

From what I could hear, this lady was the daughter of a former English Colonel, who, being a passionate hunter, had left the service and joined the Hudson Bay Fur Company. For years he lived in the far West of Canada as a nimrod, and there married a very pretty Indian squaw, daughter of a chief, and known as "The Princess." When quite young his daughter was stolen by some Indian enemy and sold to a circus manager, who had noticed her riding a wild bronco on the plains. He took her away with him to Cuba and South America, and after a time she became a most daring rider of bareback horses, and attracted much attention on account of her brilliant eyes and lovely form. Still, this is only one version of her first life, and it may not be true at all.

Knowing that she had a well-to-do aunt in Boston, she escaped one day from Havana, took passage to the States, and received a fine education from her aunt, who was delighted to have her back. When the aunt died, her niece came to visit a sister at Washington, who had married an engraver for the Government, and she soon obtained a position as greenback cutter in the Treasury Department, being so pretty and winning!

Salm met her at that time and fell in love with her, married her and took her to his camp in the field. So the Indian Princess became a German. Princess, and wife of a man whose ancestral tree went way back to the Crusaders, and who was the junior brother of a reigning Prince on the Rhine.

Besides her great beauty, the Princess was known for her remarkably free and easy manners, her determined ways and daring horsemanship, and of course other ladies considered her a mere adventuress; but in reality she was only a very shrewd woman, whose motto was the same as that of the Jesuits:

"The end justifies the means."

She was never vulgar, but blushed easily, and often showed that at heart she was a most respectable little woman. Naturally, she made use of her charms, and bestowed her favors on those who could promote her husband's interests. Proud and politely cold with ordinary men, she was seductive only with influential people and a few personal friends.

Felix Prince Salm-Salm had received a liberal education, and was one of the most high-toned and cavalier-like persons in Europe, but he was wonderfully extravagant. His generous private income as a Lieutenant in the Cavalry was soon squandered, and he contracted many debts. His wealthy brother paid these for him several times, but finally withdrew his assistance, and, pressed by creditors, the Prince was obliged to tender his resignation just when the war broke out in the States. To get rid of him, his brother bought him a passage over and advanced him a few hundred dollars in New York. Here he succeeded in becoming Colonel of the 8th New York, and behaved gallantly, but he was always in financial distress, and taxed his friends very heavily.

Like all such men, he would have been a perfect gentleman and a most charming companion if possessed of sufficient means, but situated as he was, he did many things which he would not have done had he been well off.

In spite of my kind reception and hospitality, and knowing that by his damnable appointment as Colonel in my Regiment, he had killed my well-deserved chances for promotion, he borrowed a hundred dollars from me "until next pay day." The very next morning he told me that he must create vacancies in the Regiment for seven of his friends, as he was under great obligations to them, and could only reward them by commissions in the 68th.

"They must all resign, from the Lieutenant-Colonel down," he said, "and I am glad that they received me so coolly, as this will give me an excuse for some rows."

When they had all left me on the second day, and taken quarters on the island, I meditated about how to behave, or at least, how to conduct myself. Disheartening as circumstances were, an inner voice told me: "Be clever for once in your life, and get into the good graces of the Princess. Keep clear of all intrigues, and look out for number one!"

I soon heard of some very funny scenes on the island, of quarrels, and abuse of officers, and after a short time, three lieutenants resigned, thoroughly disgusted with the treatment they had received. Three of the headquarters bummers, as we called them, were assigned to their places. But the gallant Colonel seemed not to be able to get rid of the Lieutenant-Colonel, the Major and the Captains, who all fought hard for their positions, and he had just promised these higher places to the remaining four bummers.

One day he came to me in desperation and said:

"I am in a bad fix! Those fellows I brought, or rather, had to bring along, are all without a cent. I have to feed them, keep them in cigars and wine, and it seems that I cannot drive away the higher officers. They keep away from me, but are very punctual in the performance of their duties, and speak rather impudently when I declare that I do not like to serve with them. I cannot understand, my dear Baron, how you can feel satisfied, to remain only a Captain. A man of your birth, military qualifications, past services, a regularly educated officer from Germany, magnificent rider and brave as a lion, should be at least a Colonel. Why not go East, work your influential friends, and get the Government to give you a Cavalry Regiment." I smiled sadly, and said:

"Your Highness is perfectly right, and I feel that I have not been treated very well. I came well recommended to this country as an honorably discharged officer but no one took any interest in me, and I have no friends East. I am a poor orphan in a foreign land. My bravery was called foolhardiness, my title injured me with some

German Generals, and my ambition to get promotion is dead. I am remarkably comfortable here as an independent Commander, under your orders, and my officers and men respect me, as I enforce the discipline and behavior of the regular army. You see, situated as I am, I will have no jealousy to fight, and, with the consciousness that I have acted gallantly on all occasions, and performed the trifling duties entrusted to me most faithfully, I feel happy and contented. Like you, I entered the army hoping to become a historical person, but such chances are past, for there are too many native born Americans who fight for distinction, and, worthy or otherwise, succeed by influence. If you feel friendly towards me, let me quietly guard these bridges and do not entangle me in intrigues and quarrels in the Regiment."

He said no more, but pensively mounted his horse and rode away. "Look out," I said to myself, "in his desperate state of mind he will be after your scalp, too. Do something more to secure your position!"

CHAPTER VIII.

I had been, all the time, on terms of the most friendly nature with the Princess; had driven her often in the buggy with the smart little mule, which was now only slightly lame, had escorted her on horseback, and presented her with many tokens of friendship; the freshest eggs, the best spring chickens, and the finest vegetables I could get from the farmers, had found their way to her table; but all this seemed to be insufficient.

"I must arrange a big feast in her honor," I thought, so I drew on my bank for another five hundred dollars. Then I asked that magnificent officer of the staff of General Thomas, Baron von Schrader, to procure for me the General's permission to practice my men in a sham defense of my blockhouse, and then issued printed invitations to General Thomas and his staff, to General Steed-man and staff, to Colonel Prince Salm and his ladies, and to a few officers stationed around me, to attend a

"Sham Defense of Blockhouse Number I., on the Tennessee River,

And a Banquet in honor of Her Highness, the Princess Salm-Salm."

I drilled my willing men with energy, notified all Detachments on the road to Chattanooga and Stevenson that firing at my blockhouse from four to six, on November 15, 1864, was only for the sake of practice, cleaned up the grounds thoroughly around my blockhouse, had the cottage painted and decorated with flags and flowers, and received my guests in a brand new uniform, and with my best manners.

After serving cocktails, I had an alarm sounded and asked the guests to follow me at a run to the blockhouse, which was closed and barricaded at once, and one minute later firing commenced.

The six guns, although manned by Infantry soldiers, fired with great precision at targets, placed twelve hundred yards away, all the other men fired through the loopholes, an officer placed way on top, called out the effect of the firing, and we all acted as if determined that no force of men could capture our stronghold.

The smoke inside became so dense that neither the women nor the men could breathe easily, and Tom was kept busy handing around handkerchiefs wet with cologne, and soon I had to declare the siege off, headed my command for a sally outside and drove the enemy, first by shots and then by a bayonet charge, into the wooded hills nearby.

Returning with the command in good order, I reported to Colonel Salm that the bridges were safe again, and the enemy routed, which he then reported to the superior officers.

In two tents—one for the ladies and one for the officers—toilet accommodations had been provided, and brand new tin basins and gorgeous looking-glasses gave everybody an opportunity to wash and fix up. Then we entered an immense hospital tent, loaned to me by the Chief Quartermaster at Nashville. All my guests were seated at a large table, covered with snow white linen, porcelain plates, fine glassware, napkins, etc., loaned to me for the occasion by a hotel man in Nashville.

A lovely doll formed the centre piece, representing, and actually resembling the Princess, with her big eyes, such as Byron gave to his Haidee, and Poe to his lost Leonora, with cheeks that reflected the glow of health, and a costume that showed all the refinement of fashionable society. She was surrounded by beautiful flowers, and excited much admiration.

But now came the main surprise: Twenty soldiers, in white jackets, served the repast, prepared by Mr. Sutter, once chef to the Prince of Nassau, but at present a private soldier, and acting as my cook. Oysters, consommé, with delicious little balls floating in it, fish patties, roasted wild turkeys, salads, preserves, and a rich dessert, French coffee and fine cigars. Sherry, *Pontet Canet*, Rhine wine and champagne had been served with the dishes, in turn. I now proposed a flattering toast to the health of the Princess, spoke of her curved lips:

"Red as sweet blossoms rare,

So rich in mirth When smiles were there,"

93

and so on, and all rising, shouted three hurrahs to the lovely woman's success and health.

Then drums and fifes announced that my men had marched in line, and I gave an exhibition drill, which astonished the old warriors, every one of my men being most anxious to do me honor. To my surprise, the men afterwards invited us to look at some military tableaux; one represented me when I jumped over a twenty-pound shell at Gettysburg; another, when in the act of cutting off the hand of a rebel, who had seized my bridle, and then, one of all the men charging down a hill, headed by a counterfeit of myself, leading them against the enemy and on to victory.

At dark the grounds were illuminated with Chinese lanterns, and cold supper was served in the tent, with milk punch, made of applejack and milk from my two cows. While everybody sipped this treacherous drink, some of the men sang love songs, accompanied by a guitar, and fortunately, as the evening was cool, only a few of the guests had to be sent to the trains in ambulances.

I had hardly drunk one glass during the whole evening, and was ready in case my services should be required as a commander. The Generals noted this, and complimented me, at the same time expressing' delight over the whole entertainment.

The dear Princess was the last to leave. She went in the celebrated buggy, transformed for this day into a bower of roses. She thanked me several times, and took a very affectionate leave of me at the Pontoon Bridge, the outskirt of my post.

"I will stick to you through thick and thin," she said. "Just come to me when you get into trouble!" I sighed, as if desperately in love, and kissed her delicate hand.

It took me some time to pack up things again, and to make the picnic grounds look like a dangerous fort, and not until three o'clock did I stretch myself on my bed in the cottage, for a little rest. At noon an orderly saluted me, and handed me an order from the island. It read:

"Major Kummer is hereby ordered to inspect the thirty days' rations of blockhouse number I., commanded by Baron von Fritsch, at three o'clock to-day.

Signed, Von Steinhausen.

"Lieut.-Colonel Commanding Regiment, pro tem."

I laughed outright, signed the order, and told the man to say that I would be pleased to see him. It turned out that Salm and the Princess had left at six o'clock with General Thomas for Nashville, and the uninvited officers and bummers had suspected that most probably I had used the thirty days' rations I was obliged to keep in store for my men in case of siege, in exchange for country products consumed at the banquet, and here was a chance to make charges against me.

It had most luckily happened that only a few days before the Commissary had condemned some of my rations and had sent me fresh sugar and good crackers for those damaged in the damp cellar of the blockhouse, and I had on hand not alone thirty days' good rations, but thirty days' damaged ones besides. I had never thought of even exchanging the old rations, but was in the habit of buying, at Bridgeport, such articles as I used for trading purposes.

Punctually at three the Major arrived, in full dress uniform, and I received him as a superior, with the most exaggerated display of politeness, escorted him myself to the underground cellars and furnished plenty of help to weigh the crackers, coffee, sugar, bacon, etc., handing him a list of the amount I should have on hand. When he found two hundred pounds of sugar more than I needed I could not help smiling, and left him alone with my men to discover further overweights. When he finally climbed upstairs to the main hall, I had my men drawn up in line, presented arms, and he saluted, looking ridiculously awkward. Then, with hurried steps, he crossed the bridge, while the Detachment gave three rousing cheers for me, their respected Commander.

This was the only official call I had during all the months I commanded that post and I needed no inspector, for everything was in the finest order.

The road, with its bridges, was always perfectly well guarded and never in danger, as I was on the qui vice day and night. I could have defended myself against an overwhelming force, and there was little danger in case the enemy should set fire to the blockhouse, which was always damp, and too strong to burn easily.

This mean and undeservedly suspicious act of the Lieutenant-Colonel put an end to all social intercourse with the officers on the island. I never crossed the bridges, and when an officer of the 68th called unofficially, my orderlies were instructed to deny me.

On December 18th the dear Princess, who had frequently spent a few hours with me, while her husband was hunting on my side of the river, sent for the buggy to bring her over to see me. As soon as she was comfortably seated in the easy-chair she called her own, she said:

"Baron, I have great news for you. The Prince has obtained permission from General Steedman to act as volunteer aid to him during the battle now raging near Nashville, and General Steedman has promised me, that, as soon as more troops are needed in front— if the railroad is in no immediate danger—he will form a brigade for the Colonel out of the regiments guarding from Stevenson up towards Chattanooga, and ask General Thomas to appoint him Brevet-Brigadier. Besides that, should General Thomas win the battle, Salm and this new Brigade would be used to follow up the retreating enemy. So be prepared to move at a moment's notice." Then she added: "When the Prince gets to be a full Brigadier, I promise you that I will go at once to Albany and ask the Governor to make you Colonel of the 68th Regiment, as I hate that old Lieutenant-Colonel, and the Major should be discharged for having acted so meanly towards you. I will explain all to the Governor, and I invariably succeed when I put my war paint on."

"You mean when you smile and give a kiss," I impudently remarked. "No one could refuse you anything then!"

"I'll try it," she said, smilingly. "Make me a present of that mule and buggy."

"With the greatest pleasure, Princess, but, remember, that the mule belongs to the Government, and the buggy to a farmer, who must have it back when we go away."

"All right, transfer the outfit to me, and I will be responsible for it."

"It is transferred. Anything else?"

"Well, here, you naughty boy," and I received my reward [a kiss].

I was glad to get rid of the turnout, which I had kept only for her, and after she had driven gaily away, I said to myself: "Never mind, Marie; let me achieve the rank of Colonel through a woman's influence, as I could not get it by gallantry on the battlefield. Many a knight has been promoted by a woman's favor in the good old times. No shame in that!"

At three the next morning I was sleeping in an easy-chair in the cottage, all dressed, as the blockhouse was very cool and damp that night, when I heard a challenge on the bridge: "Halt, who goes there?"

"An Orderly, with the countersign, and an order for the commanding officer."

I got up and read:

"You will report with your Command, on the island, at seven o'clock, ready to march, and with five days' rations. Von Steinhausen.

"Lieutenant-Colonel Commanding Regiment."

"Aha, he has to make Salm a Brigadier, and myself Colonel. Three cheers for the lovely Indian-German Princess!"

"Officer of the guard, wake up all the men, and say that we will march at a quarter to seven, sharp, with five days' rations. All the tents must be removed and stored, with such articles as the men cannot carry on forced marches, in the storage room of the blockhouse."

I packed up everything, keeping only one rubber blanket to be carried on my shoulders, and sent my servant, Tom, with Caesar, over to my friend, the Regimental Quartermaster, with a request that he should take both along with him. At six an artillery officer arrived with four guns, and showed me an order that he was to take charge of the post. I called my outposts in and entrusted to his care my cows, hens and the cottage furniture, and he was delighted to meet with such unexpected comforts.

At a quarter before seven I reported with my Command, and then took charge of Company A, 68th New York, temporarily, as the Princess, in bidding me farewell, had whispered to me that Salm would at once detail me on his staff.

At eight o'clock the regiment left for Stevenson, and there we heard that General Thomas had gloriously won the Battle of Nashville, on December 15th and 16th, and that we were to pursue General Hood's fleeing army.

"That's three days ago," I said to myself. "We'd better make haste!"

We were hurried by rail and steamboats to a spot near Decatur, Alabama, in the most terrific weather. It was cold, and a heavy rain was pouring down. I had stood the whole night shivering near an open fire at Stevenson, and now was kept only tolerably warm by being squeezed in among a lot of wet men.

When we were ordered to land, a Confederate battery began firing at our boat, but fortunately too high, and rushing out I stepped into a big swamp, and sank to the hips. They helped me out with fence rails, and I at once superintended the building of a fence-rail bridge, over which we hurried the men to higher ground.

The Battery retired several hundred yards, and we were fired at by some hundred Cavalrymen, who must have been armed with rifles, and supported the Battery. Salm now appeared for the first time, and I said: "You'd better send me ahead with the skirmish line, sir." "Yes, please take your Bridgeport Command and advance at once."

A cheer from my mien followed, and I deployed them in double quick and marched forward. My orders were to fire often and to try

98

to kill some Battery horses, and "those vagabonds on horseback!" So a lively fire was maintained, we marching on at a double quick, and the men halting from time to time to fire.

Coming close to the Battery, they fired grape shot once, but I had already ordered my skirmishers to lie down flat. Soon the Battery was hitched up again, and moved a thousand yards further away, we following up at once.

I noticed one horse killed and two men were shot from off their horses as we came nearer; and the Battery, after firing a few- shells over our heads, got ready to start once more.

Still I urged my men to fire rapidly and accurately, and down went another horse. The enemy had to stop that Battery, throw the horse out and, with loud hurrahs, we ran towards it, and killed two cannoniers; but with three horses, the gun escaped, passed by the earth-works before Decatur, and entered the town, the Cavalry men chasing ahead of it for their lives.

My orders from Salm had been to advance within five hundred yards of the forts and intrenchments, and to rest there till morning, when Steedman's Command would be ready to advance and charge.

I was about four hundred yards from the works, and noticed no life in them at all, so I ordered my men to lie down and rest, and, calling on Marie to protect me, I ran forward alone and peeped inside of the first large redoubt. Not a soul was there and no guns, nothing but a few rags. Jumping on the parapet, I signaled, with my sword, for the men to advance, and with loud cheering they reached me.

I now dispatched Sergeant Ricklefsen back to Salm, to report that the works and intrenchments were unoccupied, the Battery and its escort chasing through the town, and that I would advance, clear the town, and place my skirmish line on the other side, as outposts.

From the citizens I obtained information that Hood had left two days before, and that I had driven away his last rear guard. After seeing that all was safe and as it was becoming very dark, I set fire to an old barn on the outskirts to show Salm the way, and by nine that night he came, marching into town with his Brigade.

Right after him came a Negro Brigade. As their skirmishers passed me I told them to connect on both sides with my men and remain as outposts. Salm looked excited when we met, put his arms around me and said:

"Baron, you advanced bravely; many thanks!" He gave me a little brandy and a cigar, as I was, of course, terribly exhausted. Then he said:

"Turn the outposts over to a junior Captain now and stay with me, as an Inspector-General, on my Staff."

I hunted for good quarters for Generals Steedman and Salm, and selected a good lounge for myself in a fine house where all the inhabitants had locked themselves in a cellar, except a negro girl, who promised to cook supper.

At eleven o'clock General Steedman arrived, and in my presence, the Colonel commanding the Negro Regiment said: "I took Decatur, General, and my skirmishers drove the Battery out of town." This was too much for me, and, stepping forward, I exclaimed loudly and peremptorily:

"General, that is a lie! The 68th New York entered first and drove the Battery out. At least fifteen minutes after our skirmish line was acting as outposts, the colored skirmishers reached town." Rather angrily General Steedman answered:

"It's all the same who entered first. I expected to run across a big force of Hood's here, and we found only his rear guard. In a few days we will catch up with him. Good night, I am tired," and he entered the room I had secured for him. The Colonel looked at me savagely, but never said a word.

I had lost two men killed and three wounded in the advance, and many balls had whizzed by me, but only one rifle ball, from a cavalry man, had touched me. It merely pierced the rubber blanket I wore around my shoulders with a strap.

After inspecting my wounded, I thanked the men who had advanced with me, had them relieved from outpost duty, and then hurried to my couch and slept soundly for six hours, the first time I had rested in three days.

Our horses had arrived in the morning, and Tom had an overcoat for me in the saddle, so when we resumed the pursuit, I was well fixed and rode next to Salm, dreaming of future success, promotion and the lovely Princess.

In forced marches we hurried on. The next day we found two guns with broken wheels, in the woods, and later on some dead horses on the road. We captured some stragglers of the rear guard, and found some Confederates half-starved and perfectly exhausted lying under a big tree. But Hood had too good a start, and I gave up all hope of catching up with his army. General Salm thought differently, however, and chased us forward without tents and with little to eat, scarcely allowing the troops to camp at night.

The rain still poured, and the men became desperate. On Christmas Eve we halted at six o'clock, and the universal cry was:

"No coffee, no crackers!" The rain had changed to snow, which was an advantage, but the wind became still colder.

"Let us imitate Sherman," I said to Salm, "and send out foragers; I see some farms over there."

"Yes, we must have a Christmas," he assented, and volunteers were allowed to drive in all the animals they could find. Some fellows brought a whole herd of geese, others some calves, pigs and chickens, and soon we began butchering; by ten o'clock we had a bite of something.

Tom collected the feathers of the geese and made me a bed. On two sticks we fastened a rubber blanket, another one served as a cover, and Salm and I lay down, chewing some goose legs, and soon fell asleep. We awoke to find ourselves covered with snow.

On the twenty-sixth the useless pursuit was given up, and we had to march nineteen miles homeward to meet the Commissary. They furnished coffee first, and this did us much good, but we were so dreadfully exhausted that it was decided to allow us three days' rest. I managed to get a tent, and, sitting around a good fire, we soon felt better. After another hard march in beastly weather, and over almost impassable roads, we reached the railway and were shipped back to Bridgeport.

The charming Princess, after getting the order which promoted her husband to a Brevet rank, had returned to the island, where one Captain Eckert was guarding the tents and stores. With his assistance she moved the headquarters to a hill in Bridgeport proper, a much healthier location, and when we returned from our tramp, she had a good supper ready. During the evening she praised Captain Eckert very much, and expressed the wish that he should be appointed on Salm's Staff.

Eckert was a handsome, strong, young Bavarian ex-officer, who had made an impression on her, and being very unwilling to remain at headquarters and to witness all kinds of intrigues and hear of nothing but charges against this or that officer, I suggested making him Inspector and letting me go back to my cottage and farm across the river. Salm approved this, and I collected my old Command and again relieved the Artillery officer.

The railroad we guarded was now but little used, as General Sherman, after leaving Atlanta, lived upon the country supplies, and was now, I believe, punishing South Carolina. There was little danger that the enemy would destroy it and try to bum the bridges, so I had an easy time and only from time to time arranged a little scouting party up the hills to capture deserters or outlaws.

Brevet-Brigadier Salm, the hero of Decatur, was sighing for further glory, and to get Brigadier's pay, so he arranged a large expedition to search the hills after one of my scouts had reported that some rebel cavalrymen had been seen there. I obtained permission to go along mounted. After chasing some fellows, we surrounded them at night in Salm's Grove, and captured them. The report read:

"Brevet-Brigadier-General Salm-Salm, in the almost inaccessible mountains of Tennessee, fought and captured twenty of Hood's Cavalrymen (who had lost their way after the Battle of Nashville), and brought twelve horses, three mules, guns and a camping outfit to Bridgeport, Alabama."

We had had beautiful weather, and the whole trip was more like a pleasant hunting party, spiced by some little adventures.

One of mine was rather terrible. After we had surrounded the stragglers, and had made them prisoners, I was very tired and, with a Lieutenant Entress von Fürsteneck, lay in a shelter tent on a big pile of hay, with a fence-rail fire in front of us, as the night was cold.

During the night, Entress, half asleep, got up and pushed the fire nearer to the tent, as his feet felt chilled, and then went to sleep again. I was just dreaming that I was fighting a single combat with a tall, heavily bearded man, mounted on a black horse with red, fiery eyes. I cut him in two, after a long struggle, half of his body falling down on the right, the other on the left of his horse, when a powerful man tore away our tent, caught me by the collar of my overcoat and threw me a few paces away, on the ground.

I expected to be murdered right there, but then came the realization that my overcoat was on fire, and I rolled about wildly. Someone threw a blanket over me, and tried to extinguish the flames.

It was a terrible moment until I got my senses back. It turned out that our hay, tent and clothes bad caught fire, and the Sergeant of the Guard, seeing the smoke, had saved me.

I had taken off my boots before lying down, and they were all burned, so I had to ride home with my feet wrapped up in pieces cut from a rubber blanket.

Another little adventure I had was while sleeping, later on, in my cottage. Poor Sutter, my cook, had died in a hospital from fever, and I had hired a big, fat country girl to take his place. She did not cook well at first, but was willing and improved rapidly.

She resided in a partition of my barn, and always retired early. One night when the moon was full, she left her quarters, entered my room, stepped over the chairs, and then over me. When she got on my bed it woke me up, and I saw this vision dressed all in white. I stared and stared, and in the shadowy light thought for a moment that it must be Marie, but as I became thoroughly awake I called out: "Hello, there! What is that?"

This awoke her, and she fell heavily on the floor. The poor girl was a somnambulist. I did not become grey from the shock, but I felt rather uncomfortable for a few moments, and after that always locked my door.

CHAPTER IX.

As "All was quiet on the Potomac," once under McClellan, so all was quiet on the Tennessee, now under Salm. Two of his bummers, as they could not reach their desired rank, had returned North, and two had opened a shop in Bridgeport, selling every description of miserable stuff, for which I had no use.

They had all sorts of petty rows in the regiment, but at my post we lived in peace and I remained a strict, but well liked Commander until our Brigade was transferred to the district of Altoona.

Salm had his headquarters at Atlanta, and the 68th lay in camp nearby. I inhabited a wall tent in the camp, but did no duty, as I was determined to get on detached service at once. I spent the days at headquarters, and only slept in my tent.

One afternoon I walked over to the Courthouse, where the Adjutant-General, Captain Steuernagel, had his office. As I entered I heard some great noise inside. To my horror and indignation I saw the Captain on the floor and a large, light, colored woman beating him with a broomstick, and using the most outrageous language, claiming that he had proved unfaithful to her. I pushed the woman violently away, and, noticing that Steuernagel was pretty well intoxicated, abused him roundly, and said that he was unfit to wear the shoulder straps; that he was a brute, etc. When he lifted himself up he foolishly rang a bell and the Provost Marshal entered.

"Arrest that man," he shouted, "and take him to his tent under guard!"

I did not know the officer, but I said:

"All right, take me away from this den," so followed by a guard, I was escorted to my tent, and Lieutenant-Colonel Steinhausen and Major Kummer were notified that I was under arrest by order of the Adjutant-General.

Of course they were delighted, and Kummer ordered the officer of the day to place two sentinels before my tent, and to instruct them to fire if I tried to escape. I laughed right out, and, sending my servant

Tom for paper and ink, I wrote out charges and specifications against Captain Steuernagel, and sent them at once to Prince Salm with a private note.

This Captain was the same who had ordered his men to fire at me at Chancellorsville, when I returned from a reconnoitre, followed by Confederate Cavalry, and somehow or other I had hardly met him since, as at Bridgeport he was generally drunk, and if I hated anything it was a drunken officer, in charge of a detachment. He commanded a small fort on a hill above my blockhouse, but never once stopped to see me, when passing over the bridges.

Salm had appointed him Adjutant-General, as he was, when sober, a clever penman, but he never liked him, and was now glad to be rid of him. A Court was in session to try some other officers, and my charges were at once acted upon. Captain Steuernagel was dismissed from the service, the Lieutenant-Colonel and the Major were strongly rebuked for their foolish zeal, and I was honorably discharged from arrest.

The next day General H. M. Judah, commanding the district, came to Atlanta, and after a consultation with Salm and me, appointed me President of a Military Court to sit at Marietta, Georgia, for the purpose of trying such persons as should be brought before us. We had for the most part cases of planters against former slaves, some outlaws, etc., and for four months I resided at the elegant residence of Mr. Howell, a once rich planter, who had a most charming family, and they made my evenings delightful.

All our cases were appealed by Southern lawyers, and were to be tried again by civil authorities, after the war was over. I made no enemies at Marietta, and had rather an interesting time, as our Judge Advocate, Lieutenant-Colonel Alexander G. Hawes, was a remarkably bright man.

Scarcely was I installed at Marietta, which is only a few miles by rail from Atlanta, when I had a call from Captain Eckert. He had been dismissed long since as Inspector-General, on account of incompetency, as the man could scarcely speak English. He was much excited and said:

"Baron, please help me; I am in a terrible fix!" He then confided to me that he was full of whiskey on the Fourth of July, came back to camp late at night, singing German songs, and was harshly told by the officer of the day to shut up and go to bed, as he was disturbing the whole camp.

Insulted by such a speech from a younger officer, he quarreled with him, and finally struck him, after which he was arrested and kept in the guardhouse. The Lieutenant then made charges against him, and he feared dismissal from the service.

"Please act as my counsel of defense," Eckert said, "and save me."

I had noticed the Captain at Chancellorsville. He was one of the Volunteers who went out with me over the rifle-pits, on the third day, and I had seen him act very bravely at Gettysburg, so I thought him a gallant fellow, and liked him, while on the other hand, I had had several opportunities to find the Lieutenant a sneaky sort of fellow, who had been for two years on signal service, and was only recently commissioned in the Regiment. So I said:

"All right, Eckert, I will do my best to save you, as you were a brave soldier; let me know when your case will be tried." A few days later he telegraphed to me:

"Please come tomorrow." I adjourned my court, and started at once, got a hundred officers and men to testify to the Court that Captain Eckert had served from private up to Captain of Company E with great gallantly, that he had distinguished himself in several battles, had never been seen intoxicated before, and that he was a good officer and perfect gentleman. Then I brought witnesses to testify against the character of the officer of the day, and read my speech for the defense. The main point I made was that such a gentleman as Eckert had a right to get full and merry on the glorious Fourth, particularly on a Fourth when the war was over, that in 1863 he had not been full, but lay wounded and worn out on Cemetery Hill, and then ended with some funny remarks which made the whole court laugh. They retired and brought a verdict of not guilty, and the young man who had cut me out for a while in the graces of lovely Princess Salm was safe.

This success made me very popular at once, and I heard officers from the regiment frequently remark:

"It is a shame that the Captain cannot be promoted," and one afternoon a committee waited on me and presented a certificate, the copy of which can be found in the appendix. The speaker expressed the wish that after reading it the Governor of New York would appoint me Colonel of the Regiment, when Prince Salm had received his commission as Brigadier General.

After several months my court was permanently adjourned at Marietta, and I was: ordered to different towns in Georgia to advise the poor liberated slaves how to act. I occupied the Judge's seat in the different courthouses, and listened to many a sad tale. I took charge of some of the worst treated negroes, advised others to return to their plantations, and told them that although they were free, until things became more settled they must try to get along with their former masters. I usually gave them letters, in which I threatened justice if the masters did not make satisfactory arrangements with their former slaves, and advised them to let the negroes have part of the crop in payment for their services. I worked hard for the benefit of the colored race, and sometimes accompanied a whole gang back to the plantation to arrange personally the best terms I could get for them.

In November, 1865, the Brigade of Salm was transferred to the district of Savannah, most unfortunately with the Prince under arrest. He had been guilty of some deeds of doubtful character. I never investigated, as I have a horror of European noblemen disgracing themselves, and I was glad when he escaped justice by running away to Mexico, where he entered the service of Maximilian. He had left the dear Princess behind; I raised a collection to ship her to Vera Cruz.

News now reached me that the 68th Regiment, stationed at Fort Pulaski, would soon be mustered out, and although I might easily have joined the Freedman's Bureau, I decided to go North instead.

On the 26th I proceeded to Fort Pulaski, and as both the Lieutenant-Colonel and the Major were absent, I took command of the regiment and held three dress parades; then on the 30th of November, 1865, we were mustered out of the service, and sent by steamer to New York. There the officers were paid off for the last seven months, and I got my check all right, but on the stairs I met a big, fat, much excited man running up, and at the first corner of the street I was stopped by a policeman, who requested me to return as the Paymaster had made a mistake.

"This man," said the Paymaster, pointing to a Jew, "claims that you owe him four hundred and fifteen dollars balance due on a wagon-load of provisions you seized at Chancellorsville and distributed to the troops."

I explained that every man was responsible for what he had bought.

"Yes, but the men were paid off long ago," screamed the ex-sutler, "and where, by the holy Moses, can I find them now? You forced me to sell to them; I had to do it to save my life. Oh merciful God, how you scared me! You must pay now, or I am a ruined man."

I replied coolly: "Paymaster, deduct that amount or this fellow will never cease to annoy me. I am glad that I had a chance on that to treat the starved men of my Brigade."

"God bless you!" hallooed the Jew, and I walked off with seven months' pay, minus the four hundred and fifteen dollars.

Three days afterward I presented cards to the downtown merchants, inscribed:

VATEL & FRITSCH

Brokers and Commission Merchants

48 Pine Street, New York.

EDITOR'S NOTE

The foregoing pages have given only the war history of this remarkable soldier, but the frequent and romantic references to his guardian angel and talisman, "Marie," show a depth of devotion to the memory of an ideal as rare as it is admirable.

The Countess Marie von R., to whom Captain Von Fritsch was betrothed, was one of the most attractive, beautiful and accomplished belles of the Dresden Court circle.

Her lovely face with its exquisite coloring in its frame of golden hair, typical of her pure Saxon blood, her eyes of blue, her lips of wondrous mould and tint, her brilliantly white teeth, her symmetrical and graceful form made her the most attractive of women. It is small wonder the memory of her loveliness has given inspiration, strength and courage to a brave man, whose romantic love and fidelity must command the respect and sympathy of all who appreciate the value of deep sentiment.

The cause which separated these two loving hearts is most pathetic.

Although only in her eighteenth year the attachment between the Countess Marie and Captain Von Fritsch had been of years' standing and they determined to wed.

The marriage was fixed for the eighteenth day of September, 1856. During that summer with her mother and sister, the Countess Marie was a guest of the Baron's father, at his splendid castle, Seerhausen, near Riesa, Saxony.

Toward the end of July, the Baron secured a long leave of absence and joined the family circle. His arrival marked the beginning of a continuous round of amusements. Horse races, excursions and games of all kinds took place by day, and the nights were made delightful by balls, illuminations, or moonlight sails on the lake in the park. As a crowning diversion preparations were made for a genuine tournament, in which the Baron and some of his fellow officers, accoutered in armor, were to break lances like the knights of old.

In the midst of the preparations, while at breakfast on August tenth, the Baron was handed the following summons:

You are hereby ordered to report without delay to General von Engel at Dresden and to accompany him as aid-de-camp on a special mission to St. Petersburg. You have been selected for this special honor on account of your thorough knowledge of the French language and your approved conduct at Court.

Signed Von Rabenhorst,

Secretary of War.

The reading of this document elicited expressions of disappointment from all present and the Countess Marie, who was sitting beside the Baron, became visibly excited. In a tremulous voice she exclaimed:

"For weeks a presentiment has troubled me that something would occur to prevent our union on September eighteenth."

"Do not alarm yourself, my Marie," replied the Baron, "I will be back on or before that day! You see, my dear, a soldier must obey commands and, although it is unusual to detail an officer who is on leave of absence, the appointment will be regarded as a distinct honor, and will no doubt bring me several decorations. But no power on earth can keep me from calling you my beloved bride on the eighteenth."

"Let us see," said his excellency, the Baron's father, "they will probably start in about two days, take seven to reach Russia's capital, where they will remain scarcely more than a week, then seven days to return and, at the very latest, Otto will be back in twenty-three days. So you see he will be here during the first week in September, long before the happy day."

"May God grant it!" added the Countess Marie,' but she seemed much disturbed and was noticeably silent.

The Baron drove away the same morning after a most tender parting with Marie, and being wished *"Glückliche Reise"* by everyone present.

"*Lebewolil*, Marie!" exclaimed the Baron, as the carriage started, and he waved his handkerchief until he disappeared.

"I shall never see him again," said Marie, between her sobs!

She was inconsolable, and did not leave her room for days. At last, however, a letter arrived from the Baron announcing his departure and conveying the general's assurance that he would soon return. This restored her good spirits in a measure, and she rejoined the family circle. Nevertheless she had occasional fits of despondency and in one of these remarked:

"I cannot understand the feeling I have that we will never meet again. Even in my dreams I am warned. I see funeral processions, people dressed in the deepest mourning. What can it all mean?"

Everyone tried to reassure her, and as time wore on and cheerful letters arrived daily from the Baron, the fits of despondency became less frequent. The gloom which these forebodings cast over the family circle had been all but dispelled when a shocking event overwhelmed it with the deepest woe.

The Baron on his leave of absence had brought to the castle five fine horses and, during his last week's stay, was trying to break a well matched pair to harness. They were fiery, but under his management, docile and obedient animals. Before leaving he requested his father's veteran coachman to drive them daily for exercise.

On the morning of August 25th, the family was assembled before the castle watching the peasants fishing for carp in the fosses.

The old coachman, with the new team attached to a dog cart, drove by. Marie stopped him to ask about the animals.

"They go like lambs," he answered.

"Take me for a little drive?" she requested.

After the coachman, who had been in the family for thirty-five years, and in whom the fullest confidence was reposed, had assured the family that there was not the slightest danger, the young countess was allowed to take a seat in the cart.

Old Jacob started the horses in a walk, they crossed the square and drove into the court-yard. There, the countess opened her parasol and at the same time turned and called out to reassure her mother:

"They behave splendidly!"

Alas! Her confidence was premature. The parasol frightened the horses, they reared. The countess was frightened, but had the presence of mind to quickly close and lower the parasol. Unfortunately that had the unexpected effect of terrifying the horses still more and, after plunging wildly for a.; few seconds, they broke and ran.

Out they flew, through the gates to the main road, which turned at a short distance to the left. The horses increased their speed; the coachman, unable to check them, managed to keep them in the road and turned the bend in safety. Past the last house in the village is a bridge across a creek and beyond a wide meadow. Once safe across the bridge the horses could soon be tired out on the soft earth beyond, and to attempt that was Old Jacob's purpose. It was his only chance and bravely he struggled for it, but fate was against him. The left front wheel of the cart struck the heavy stone abutment of the bridge. The cart was instantly destroyed and the countess was thrown over the railing of the bridge into the bed of the creek, which contained little water but was filled with large rocks.

Some peasant boys who witnessed the accident ran to summon the family, who with the villagers, were soon gathered about the scene. The beautiful young countess lay on her back, while blood from her golden head stained the crystal rivulet. Strong hands lifted her tenderly and placed her on the soft meadow grass. The old village doctor knelt and examined her long and carefully. When he lifted his head tears stood in his eyes. He removed his hat and said:

"She is dead."

The effect of this crushing blow is known to all who read these interesting pages. Captain Von Fritsch became an American of the highest type. For three years and two months he fought most bravely on the Union side, as his comrades have certified and that he made an honorable record as a soldier and a gentleman cannot be denied. Unfortunately he had no chance to rise to great rank in the army, for he lacked political influence, and even his application for brevet rank, as a recognition for his gallant conduct was placed on file.

In his declining years what happiness would be his, could some such honor be given him. It may be the letter of General Howard will bring him that priceless treasure, the medal of honor, and to this accomplishment his friends must bend their energies.

During the war Captain Von Fritsch suffered more severe hardships than many other officers saw. After long marches it was his duty, as a staff officer to place the outposts and call them in early in the morning—thus making his hours of rest very short. He was injured for life, when his horse was killed by many balls at Chancellorsville, and since then rheumatism, bronchial troubles and a great toe crushed by a cannon wheel have made him a great sufferer. By his wonderful constitution, his courage and power of endurance, he was able to enter an active business life, in which, through honesty, force of character and ability, he has been successful enough to accumulate a small fortune, on the interest of which he lives a quiet and retired life, in the evenings a welcome visitor at the homes of many of our most distinguished families.

He is a member of the Military Order of the Loyal Legion of the United States, and has lately been transferred from the commandery of Illinois, to that of the District of Columbia. He is also a member of the Army and Navy Club of the City of New York as well as of several other well-known clubs in different cities of the Union.

When the Spanish [-American] War [1898] broke out he made a great effort to be commissioned once more in the volunteer army, but he again lacked sufficient political influence to bring him proper recognition.

Hardships incurred in warfare and rheumatic pains in the head and eyes compelled him to give up active pursuits a year ago, and he is spending his declining years in Washington, surrounded by memories of the past and hopes of the future. His rooms are beautified by several large American flags, and during my recent visit, when noticing this, he exclaimed with all the enthusiasm of youth:

"I love that flag and am ready to die at any time yet—defending it."

Joseph Tyler Butts.

Containing a letter from Major-General O. O. Howard and several certificates and recommendations.

District of Columbia, Washington, D. C., August 2, 1902.

I herewith certify that I have carefully examined the following Documents, numbered one to six, and have found them to be true and correct copies of the originals shown to me:

1. Certificates from the Officers of the 68th Regiment, New York Veteran Volunteers, dated Atlanta, Ga., Sept. 15, 1865.

2. Certificate from Hon. H. Claussenius, Consul of the German Empire, dated Chicago, March 1, 1878.

3. Eleven letters of Recommendations of prominent Chicago citizens, dated January 12, 1892.

4. A letter from Hon. A. Willard, U. S. Consul at Guaymas, dated January 20, 1883.

5. A letter from George M. Pullman, Esq., President of the Pullman Palace Car Co., dated November 25, 1893.

6. A letter from Major-General O. O. Howard, dated New York, November 15, 1901.

Louis C. White,

Notary Public.

P. O. Department, Washington, D. C.

Number I.

A certificate from all the officers of the 68th Regiment, New York Veteran Volunteers, attached to a petition to the Governor of New York, to honor Captain Frederick Otto Von Fritsch after a hard service of three years in the field, with the Rank of Colonel, for brave and meritorious services rendered during the War of the Rebellion.

We, the undersigned, Officers of the 68th Regiment, New York Volunteers, certify that:

Captain Frederick Otto Von Fritsch, of Company A, 68th Regt, N. Y. Veteran Volunteers, is a brave, gallant and good officer and also a perfect gentleman, that he distinguished himself at the battle of Chancellorsville by his courage and activity, and showed great presence of mind and personal courage at the battle of Gettysburg, and on other occasions.

Respectfully,

A. Von Haake, Capt. 68th Regt., N. Y. Inf.
H. W. Reissberg, Surgeon 68th N. Y. V. V.
Otto Botticher, Jr., Q. M. 68th N. Y. Y. V.
William Mussehl, Chaplain.
Carl Riese, Adjutant 68th N. Y: Y.
Jacob Weber, 1st Lt. 68th N. Y.
Max Eckert, Capt. 68th N. Y. V.
M. Entress von Fursteneck, 2d Lt. 68th N. Y.
Adolph Joseph, Com. Co. F., 68th N. Y.
William Axt, Lt. 68th Regt., N. Y. Vols.
Frank Haffner, Capt. Co. D, 68th N. Y. V.
Paul G. Botticher, 1st Lt. 68th N. Y. Yols. Inf.
Louis Thomser, 2d Lt. 68th N. Y. Vols.
Theodore Feldstein, Capt. 68th N. Y. Vols.
George Renneberg, Capt. 68th Regt., N. Y. Vols.
Heartily approved:
Felix Prince Salm, Brevet Brigadier-General.
A. Von Steinhausen, Lt.-Col. 68th Regt., N.Y. Vet. Vol.

Number II.

A Certificate of Honorable H. Claussenius, Consul of the German Empire, at Chicago.

I take great pleasure in stating that I am personally acquainted with Mr. Otto von Fritsch since December, 1856, when he first landed in New York and presented letters of recommendation to the late Consul General of Prussia. Since that Mr. Otto von Fritsch was specially recommended to C. F. Adae, Esq., formerly Consul of Saxony, etc., by the Minister of Foreign Affairs of the Kingdom of Saxony, who stated that Otto von Fritsch is the oldest son of His Excellency Baron Chas von Fritsch, who was for many years an Ambassador to the German Diet at Frankfort-on-the-Main, and who now lives retired from public life in the winter months at Nizza, and in the summer on his estate, Seerhausen, near Biesa, in Saxony.

The Secretary of State further stated that Otto von Fritsch had been educated in the Military Academy at Dresden, and served several years as an Officer in the Royal Cavalry.

Tired of military life in peace time, and anxious to visit the New World, he tendered his resignation to the King in 1856, and was honorably discharged. For several years he spent most of his time traveling for information's sake, both in the States and in the Republic of Mexico, and in 1862 he entered the Federal army as Captain of the 68th Regiment, New York V. Volunteers, serving three years and two months, most all the time detailed as a Staff Officer.

I further state that since his muster out he has been following mercantile pursuits in New York, Cincinnati and Chicago, bearing a high character for honor and integrity.

H. Claussenius,

Consul of the German Empire.

Chicago, March 1st, 1878.

Number III.

Eleven letters of recommendation from leading Chicago Citizens for a position in the Department of Foreign Affairs of the Chicago World's Fair.

Chicago, Ill., January 12, 1892.

I most cordially recommend Mr. F. O. Von Fritsch, for a position in the department of foreign affairs, believing that his extensive travel in Europe, Central and South America, his thorough command of the Spanish, German, French and Italian languages eminently fit him for any position in that department.

He is an educated and courteous gentleman, whose talents, in my opinion, will be of great value to the department to which I suggest he be assigned.

Respectfully,

William R. Page,

Attorney-at-Law.

I have known Mr. Von Fritsch for over twenty years, and I feel assured that no better man can be found to fill the position suggested by the above letter of recommendation.

Joseph Wright,

Counsellor-at-Law.

Mr. Von Fritsch was five years in my employment, viz.: from 1867 to 1872, during which period I had ample opportunity to trace his antecedents as well as to test his integrity and ability, and I cheerfully endorse all which is above written of him. S. D. Kimbark, Hardware.

I have known Mr. Von Fritsch nearly twenty years, and cordially endorse the favorable recommendations above set forth.

Henry Greenbaum,

Banker.

I am personally acquainted with Mr. O. Von Fritsch since 1861, when he entered the U. S. Union Army in N. Y. in 68th Regt., N. Y. Vol., and join gladly the above recommendations.

H. Claussenius,

German Consul.

I heartily endorse the foregoing testimonials and recommend Mr. Von Fritsch, for an appointment in the Department of Foreign Affairs. An acquaintance with him for nearly twenty years justifies my high opinion of his ability and integrity.

Walter L. Peck,

Capitalist.

Mr. Von Fritsch seems to me to be well qualified for the position which he seeks.

Feed. W. Peck,

Director, World's Fair.

I heartily concur in the recommendations herewith, believing that Mr. Von Fritsch is competent to discharge the duties mentioned, but also that his extensive travels and familiarity with foreign languages tend to assure that his efforts would be crowned with success.

A. F. Seeberger,

Treasurer, World's Fair, Chicago.

Mr. E. J. Gage,

President of the World's Fair, Chicago.

Dear Sir: I beg hereby to endorse the application of Mr. F. O. Von Fritsch for a position in connection with the World's Fair. His application and credentials are, I believe, on file with Director-General Davis. I have been acquainted with Mr. Von Fritsch for fifteen or twenty years, and know him to be an educated gentleman well fitted by ability and experience to fill important positions. If he is appointed to the desired position he will, I am sure, acquit himself in a manner that will reflect credit upon the Directory and himself.

Yours respectfully,

Philip D. Armour.

Kindly referred to Col. Geo. R. Davis.

L. J. Gage, President.

Office of the Illinois Staats-Zeitung Co., Chicago, January 15, 1891. Hon. George R. Davis.

Dear Sir: It gives me great pleasure to endorse the application of Mr. Von Fritsch for an appointment under you. I have known Mr. Von Fritsch for many years and believe him to be the very man for the position he seeks.

His acquaintance with many countries, his knowledge of several languages admirably fit him for this appointment.

Yours respectfully,

Washington Hesing.

United States Depositary,

New Orleans, July 4, 1891. Hon. Walker Fearne,

Chicago, Ill.

Dear Sir: I take great pleasure in presenting to you my friend, Baron F. O. von Fritsch. He is a gentleman of intelligence and culture, and is, I believe, an applicant for a position in your department for which he is eminently qualified.

Your attention to my request will be much appreciated by

Yours very respectfully,

A. Baldwin.

Number IV.

Unsolicited letter from Honorable Alexander Willard, U. S. Consul at Cucymas, Mexico.

Consulate of the United States of America at Guaymas, Mexico.

January 20, 1883.

Col. F. O. von Fritsch, Agt, S. R. R. Co. (L) Hermosillo.

My dear Col.: I am in receipt of your note of yesterday in which you inform me of your intention of severing your connection with the Sonora R. R. Co., after three years of constant and efficient service rendered in the engineering and transportation service of the company.

Without discussing the reasons which have caused you to voluntarily sever your connection with the Co., I can say that I regret it; and if any word from me as to your fidelity and activity be needed let me know.

You have my best wishes always, wherever you may go. Your sincere friend,

A. Willard.

Number V.

Letter from George M. Pullman, Esq., President of Pullman's Palace Car Company.

Pullman's Palace Car Company,

OFFICE OF THE PRESIDENT.

Chicago, November 25, 1893.

Baron Otto von Fritsch,

Hotel Florence, Pullman, Ills.

My dear Baron: Your final report as Manager of our exhibit at the World's Columbian Exposition was received while I was absent in the East.

I feel that something more than a mere acknowledgement of its receipt is due you, and I take pleasure in expressing the Company's appreciation of your valuable services.

The position which you occupied in so conspicuously representing our interests, was an important and peculiarly trying one, involving constant vigilance and attention to details, and its varied requirements were met by you with commendable dignity and with credit to the company.

Very truly yours,

G. M. Pullman,

President.

Number VI.

A letter from Major-General Oliver Otis Howard. Gen. O. O. Howard, Managing Director,

150 Nassau St., New York.

LINCOLN MEMORIAL UNIVERSITY.

November 15, 1901.

Capt. Frederick Otto Baron von Fritsch, Bensonburst, L. I.

Dear Captain: Your kind letter to Col. Adams has been referred to me. This is the first time that I had any realizing sense that you were the one who helped me to mount after my horse fell over at Chancellorsville. I stayed some little time after that before I retired to make a new formation at the edge of the timber, then I rode back to the rising ground near Chancellorsville, where the corps was reformed. With all my heart I thank you for the assistance you rendered me. To risk one's life for another is the greatest favor that a man can confer. I hope you are well, and that at some time you will call in and see me and talk the matter over. It must have been due to the extraordinary excitement of the occasion that I did not take in your rank and remember your name. Very sincerely your friend,

Oliver Otis Howard, Major-General,

U. S. Army, once commanding the Eleventh Army Corps.

Office of La Belle Creole Factory,

New Orleans, La., June 20, 1890.

To Sprague, Warner & Co., Chicago, 111

Dear Sirs: We are in receipt of your favor of the 8th inst., and in reply would state, that Colonel F. O. Von Fritsch was with us for several years, and represented our house and several other large New Orleans concerns in Mexico and the Central American States, and we found him at all times to be a strictly honest, energetic and most honorable gentleman. S. Hernsheim Bros. & Co.

THE END

Discover more lost history from BIG BYTE BOOKS

Made in the USA
Middletown, DE
15 July 2019